OLSAT PRACTICE TEST

Gifted and Talented Prep for Kindergarten and 1st Grade

2014 Edition

Written and Published by
Pi For Kids Inc.

Dr. Alex Pang
Priscilla Wong
Stephanie Pang
Raymond Pang
Owen Pang

The OLSAT® is a registered trademark of NCS Pearson Inc., which is not affiliated in any way with Pi For Kids Inc. or with the OLSAT® Practice Test for Kindergarten and 1st Grade.

Pi For Kids Inc.
Queens, New York,
USA
pi4kids.inc@gmail.com

OLSAT® PRACTICE TEST

Gifted and Talented Prep for Kindergarten and 1st Grade

2014 Edition

Written and Published by
Pi For Kids Inc.

Dr. Alex Pang
Priscilla Wong
Stephanie Pang
Raymond Pang
Owen Pang

Copyright © 2014 by Pi For Kids Inc. All rights reserved. No part of this book may be reproduced or transmitted in any form or by any means, electronic or mechanical, photocopying, recording, or by any information storage and retrieval system, without written permission from Pi For Kids Inc.

ISBN-13:978-1500720483
ISBN-10: 1500720488

Pi For Kids Inc.
Queens, New York,
USA
pi4kids.inc@gmail.com

Dear Parents and Teachers,

As a parent of four children, I have experienced just how early education plays a significant role in the child's attitude towards learning for the rest of his or her life. When they are young, children are naturally curious and desire to explore everything.
At that age, their brains are developing at an incredible growth rate. With the right amount of stimuli and appropriate challenge, I believe that every child can be developed into a member of the so-called gifted and talented category. I also believe that teachers and parents hold great responsibility in establishing a setting for children in which they may have access to the greatest educational opportunities. Therefore, many states in our country have created special gifted and talented programs to allow children access to a more vigorous education.

To accept students to the programs, many school systems require children to take tests. The OLSAT, which stands for the Otis-Lennon School Ability Test, is one of the most common tests used across the country for entry into gifted and talented school programs. The test is designed to assess Verbal Comprehension, Verbal Reasoning, Pictorial Reasoning, Figural Reasoning, and Quantitative Reasoning. In more general terms, this verbal test is used to test reasoning skills and children's ability to follow the directions given to them. It is often administered with the NNAT, which is a nonverbal assessment for gifted and talented programs. However, these kinds of tests can be intimidating, especially for children who have never experienced something similar before. Therefore, an appropriate amount of practice before of the actual tests can make significant difference.

Apart from providing tools to prepare children for these standardized exams, we also want to make sure that the exercises are fun and attractive. We use colorful pictures and interactive matching exercises to help children learn the necessary ideas for the test. There is also a full length OLSAT practice exam included at the end of this book. Our goal is assist you in your journey to supporting the motivation, learning and development of your child.

Sincerely,

Dr Alex Pang
Pi For Kids Inc.

Table of Contents

Topic 1: Color and Shapes Associations __ 1

Topic 2: Completing Pattern _____ 9

Topic 3: Associations _____ 15

Topic 4: Puzzles _____ 24

Topic 5: Finding Differences _____ 33

Topic 6: Concentration _____ 39

Topic 7: Picture Analogies _____ 49

Topic 8: Visual Skills _____ 60

Topic 9: Critical Thinking _____ 68

Topic 10: Sequences _____ 74

Topic 11: Math Concept _____ 81

NNAT2 Additional Practice _____ 88

OLSAT Practice Test _____ 94

OLSAT Prompts and Answer Key _____ 105

Answer Key for Topic 1 to 11 _____ 110

Topic 1 Color and Shapes Associations

Draw lines to connect figures from the left and the right that form complete shapes.

1.
2.
3.
4.

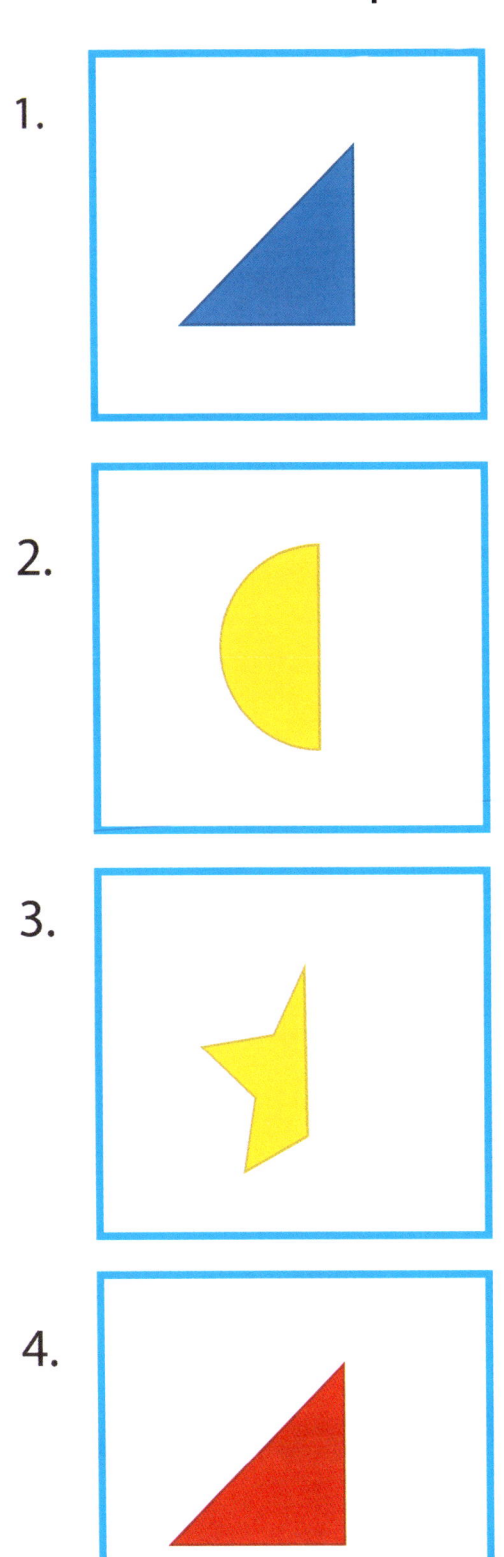
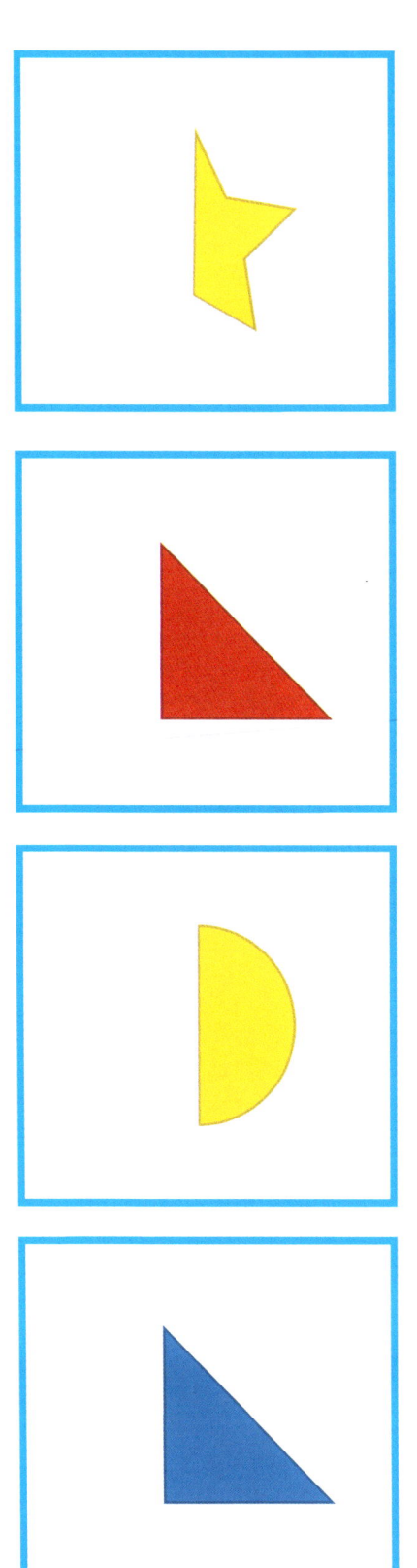

Topic 1   Color and Shapes Associations

Draw lines to connect each picture on the left to the shapes it is made up of.

5.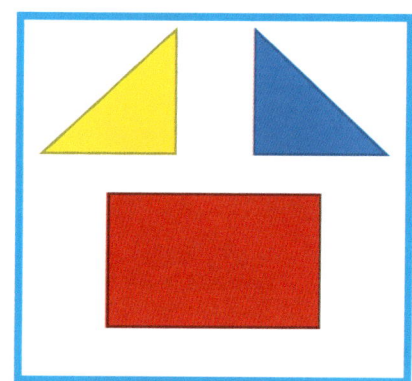

6.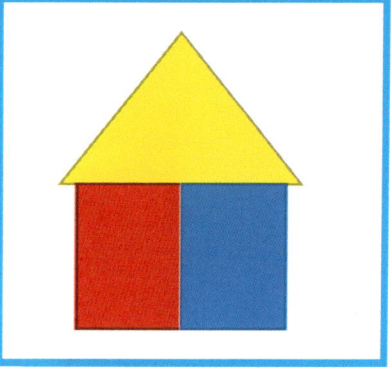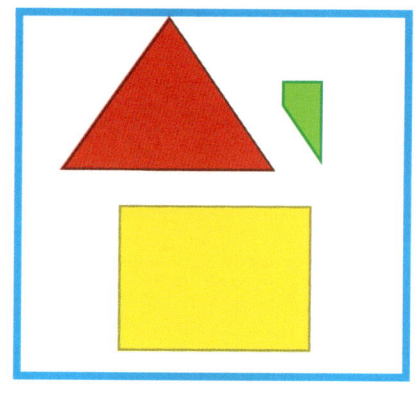

7.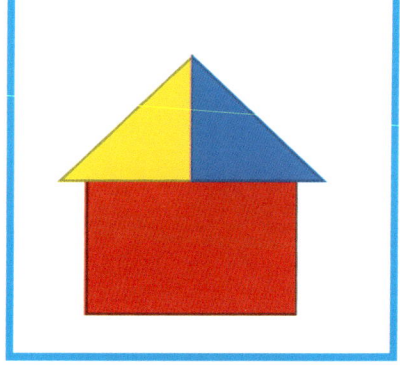

8.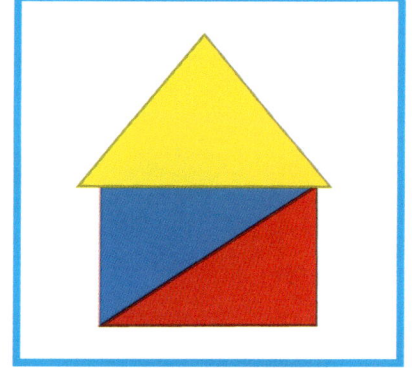

Topic 1 Color and Shapes Associations

Draw lines to connect each picture on the left to the shapes it is made up of.

9.

10.

11.

12.

Pi For Kids Inc.© OLSAT Practice Test 3

Topic 1   Color and Shapes Associations

Draw lines to connect figures from the left and the right that form complete pictures.

4   OLSAT Practice Test   Pi For Kids Inc.©

Topic 1 Color and Shapes Associations

Draw lines to connect pictures of cubes of the same size.

17.
18.
19.
20.

Pi For Kids Inc.©   OLSAT Practice Test

Topic 1   Color and Shapes Associations

Draw lines to connect each gingerbread man cookie to the pieces that it is made up of.

21.

22.

23.

24.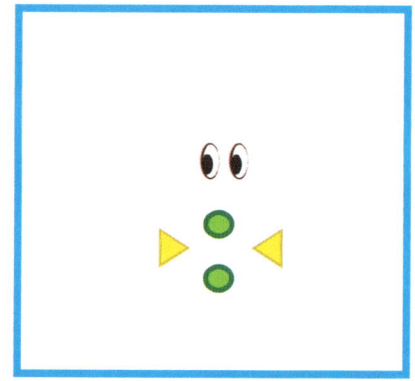

Topic 1   Color and Shapes Associations

Draw lines to connect each cookie cutter to the cookies it could be used to make.

25.

26.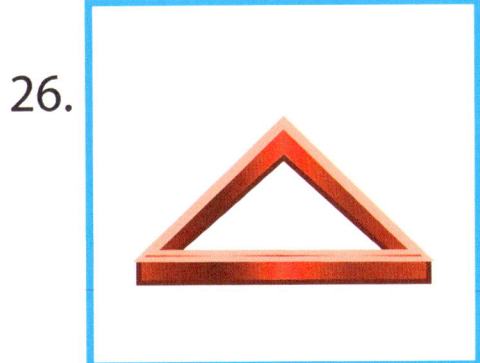

27.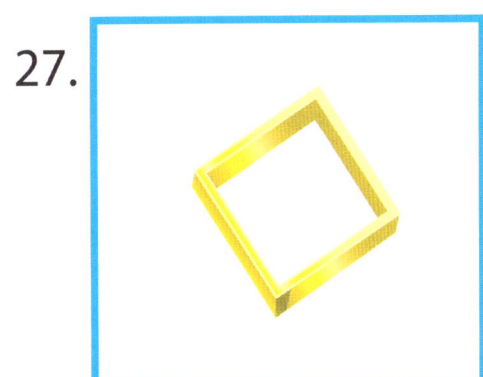

28.

Topic 1   Color and Shapes Associations

Draw lines to connect figures from the left and the right that would form complete Jack o' Lanterns.

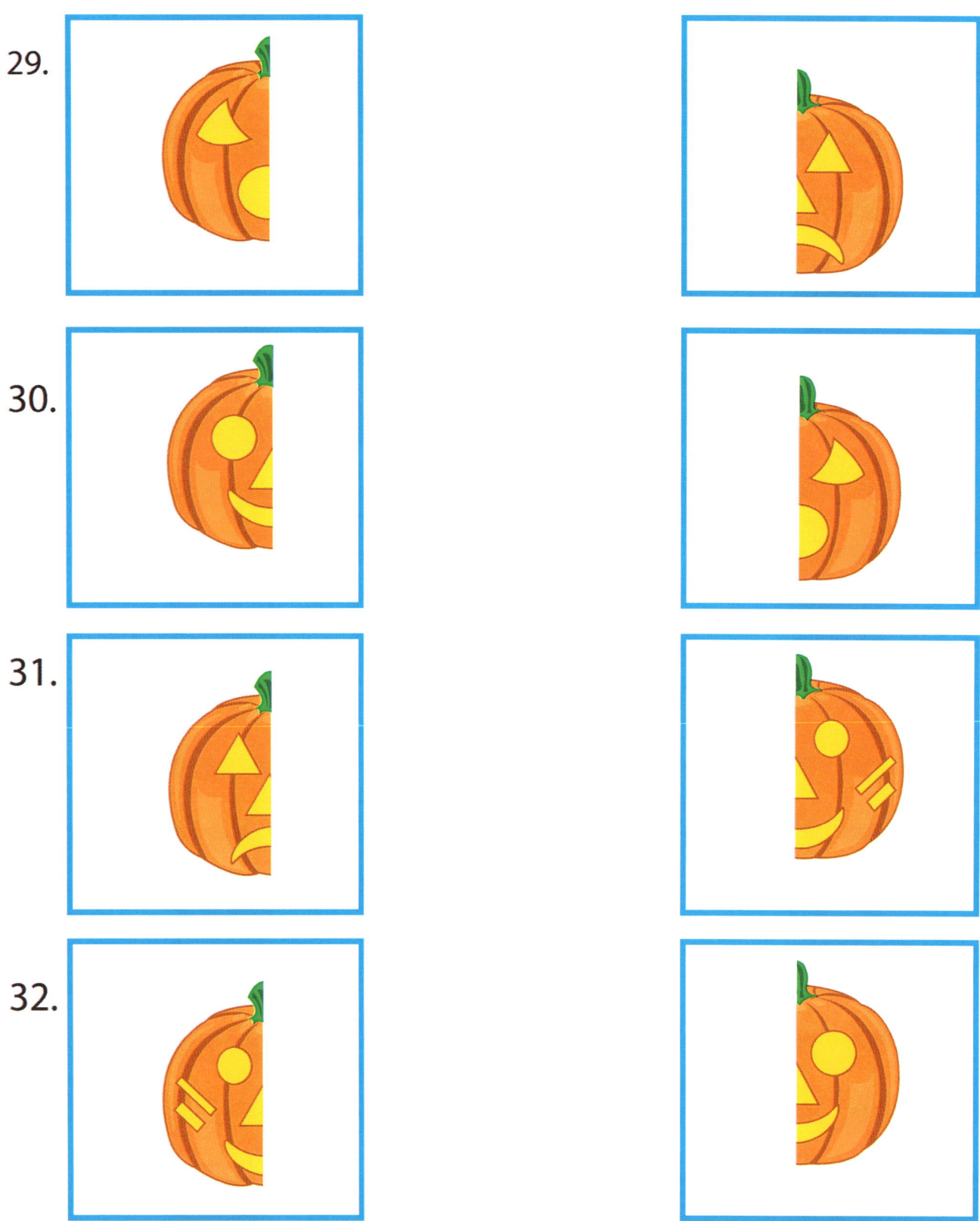

29.

30.

31.

32.

8   OLSAT Practice Test   Pi For Kids Inc.©

Topic 2 — Completing Patterns

Fill in the circle under the picture that best completes the pattern shown in each question.

1.

2.

3.

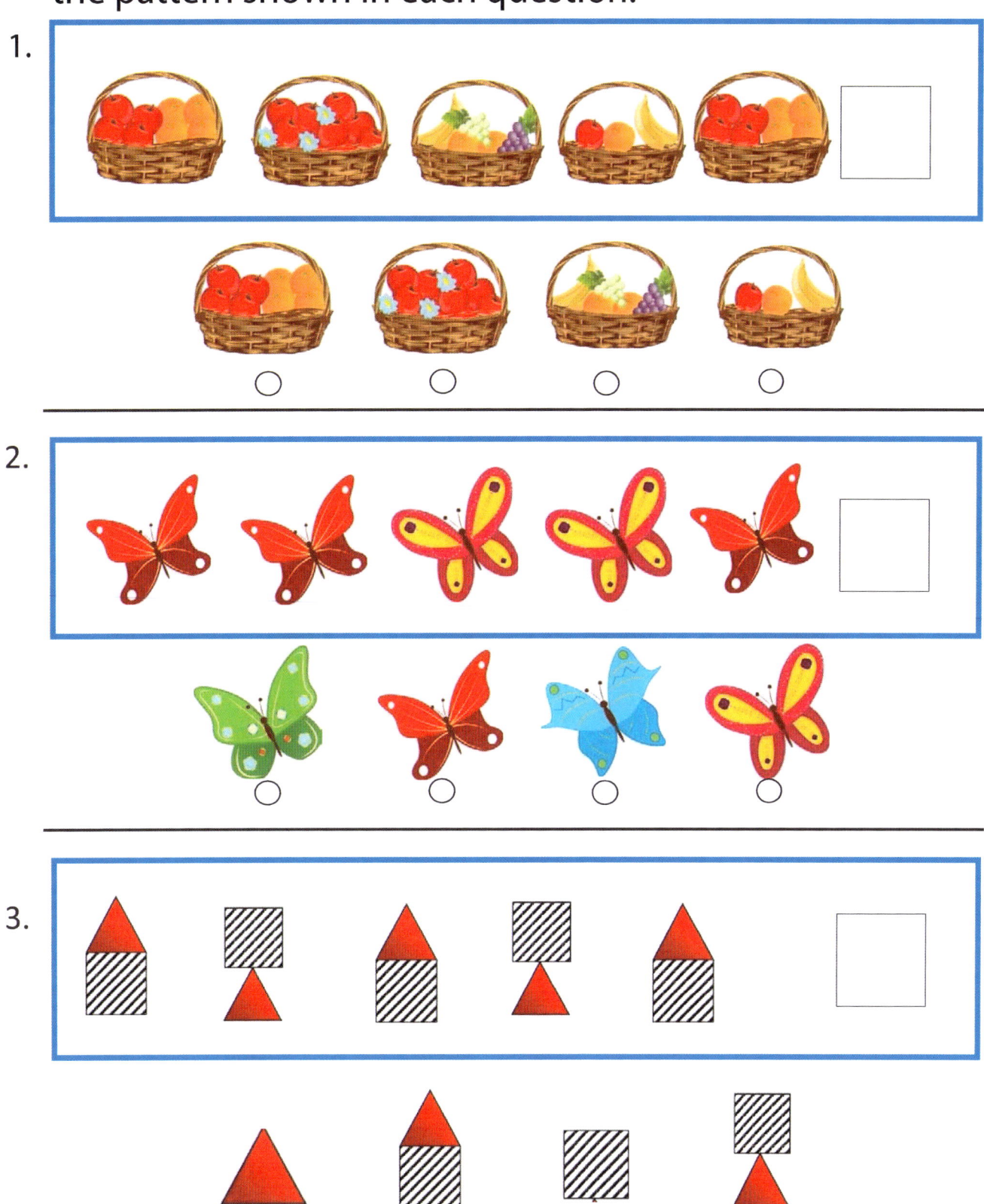

Topic 2 — Completing Patterns

Fill in the circle under the picture that best completes the pattern in each question.

4.

5.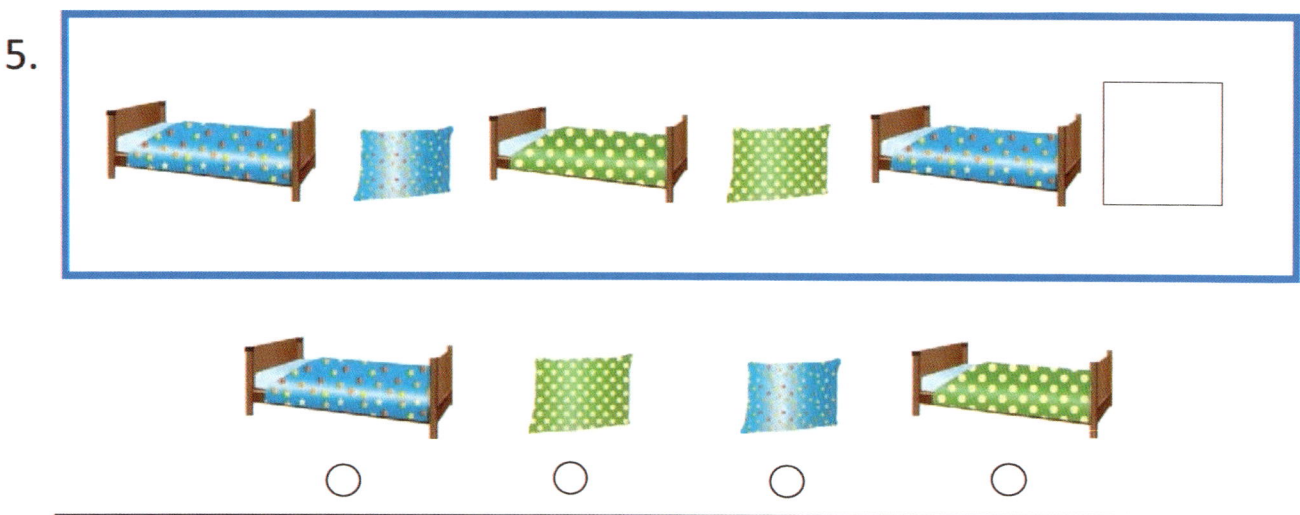

6.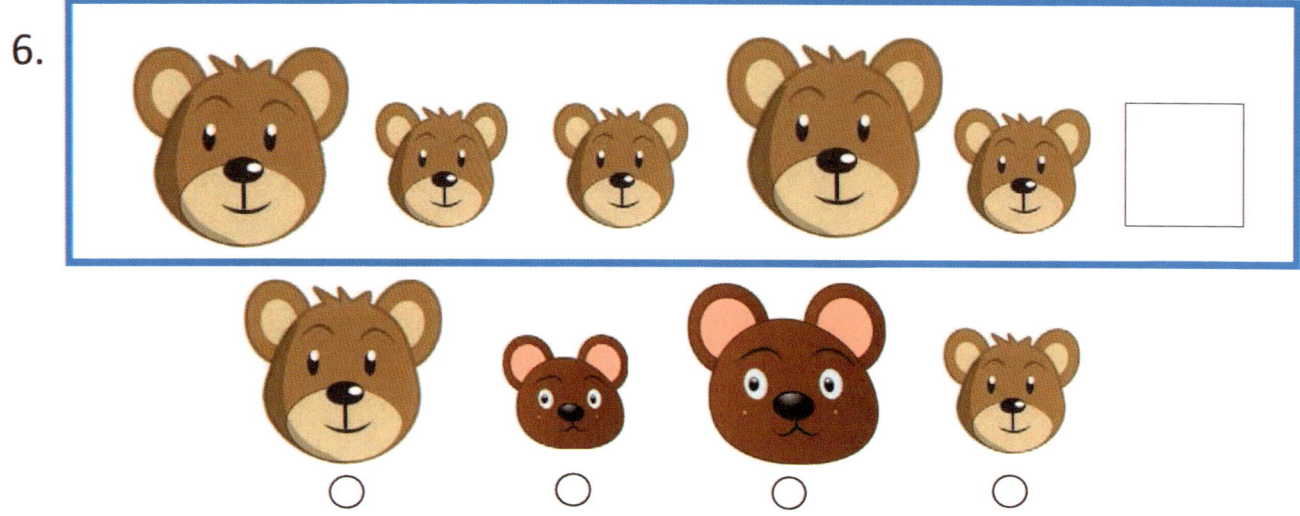

Topic 2 — Completing Patterns

Fill in the circle under the picture that best completes the pattern in each question.

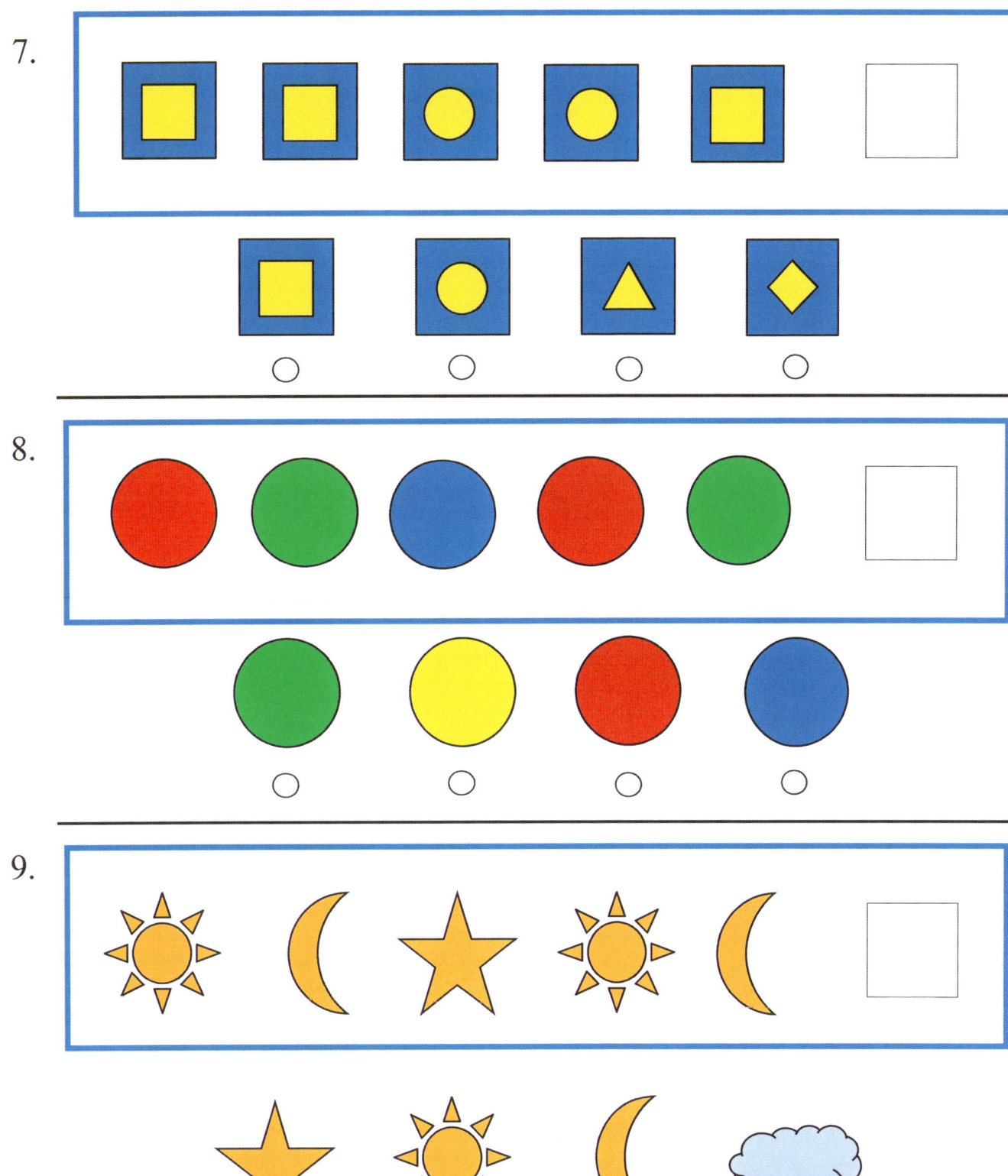

Topic 2 — Completing Patterns

Fill in the circle under the picture that best completes the pattern or story in each question.

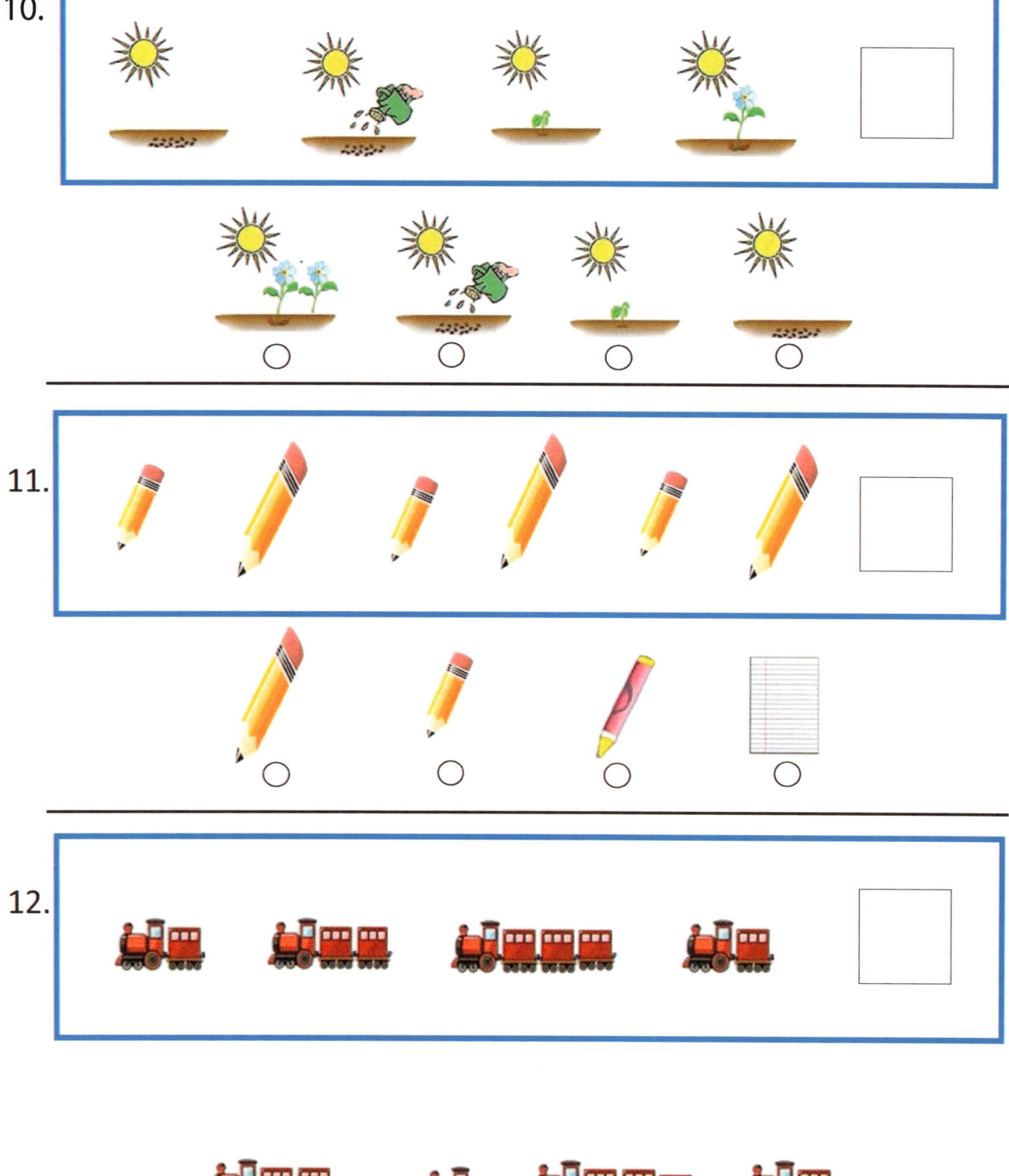

10.

11.

12.

Topic 2 Completing Patterns

Fill in the circle under the picture that best completes the pattern in each question.

13.

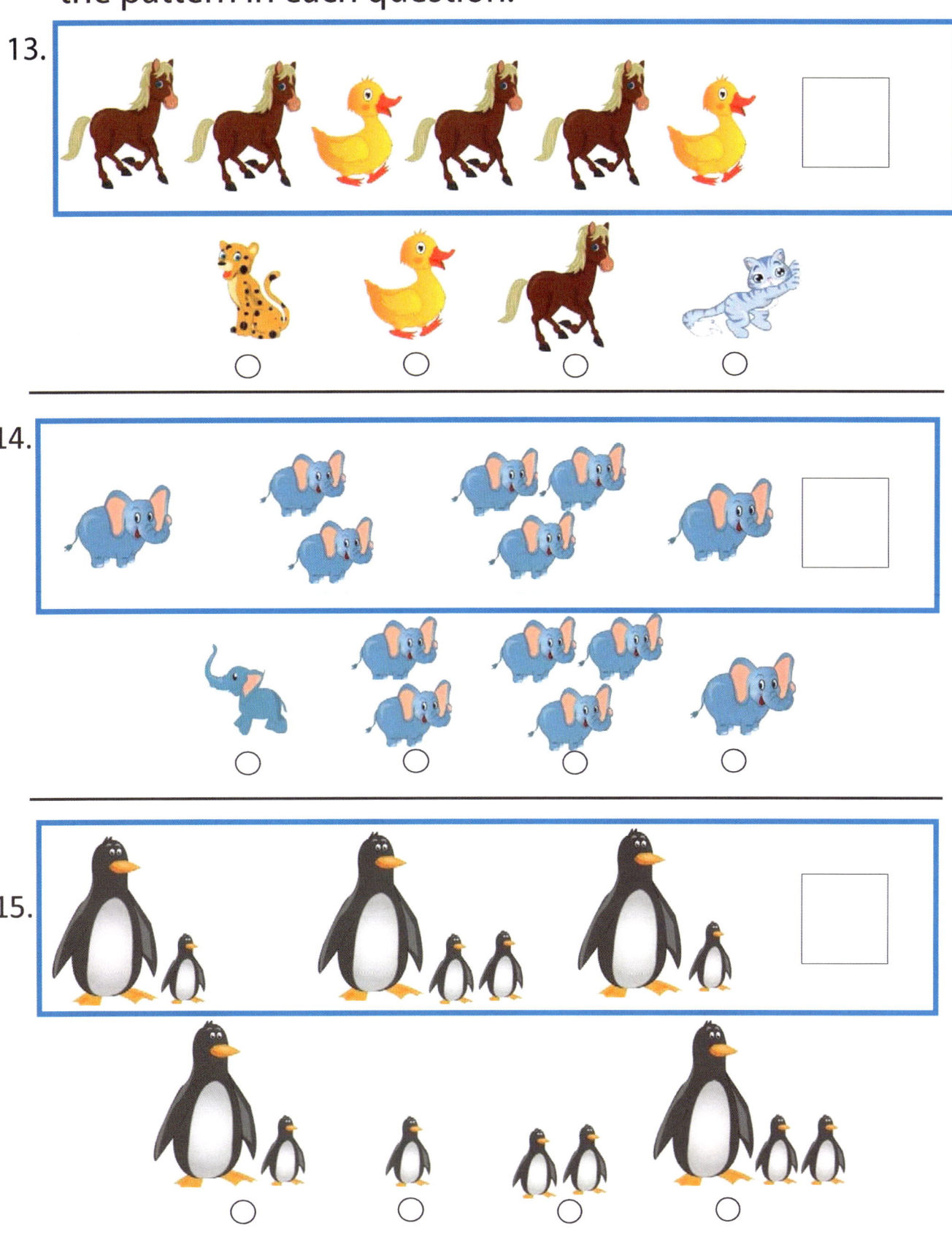

Topic 2 — Completing Patterns

Fill in the circle under the picture that best completes the pattern in each question.

16.

17.

18.

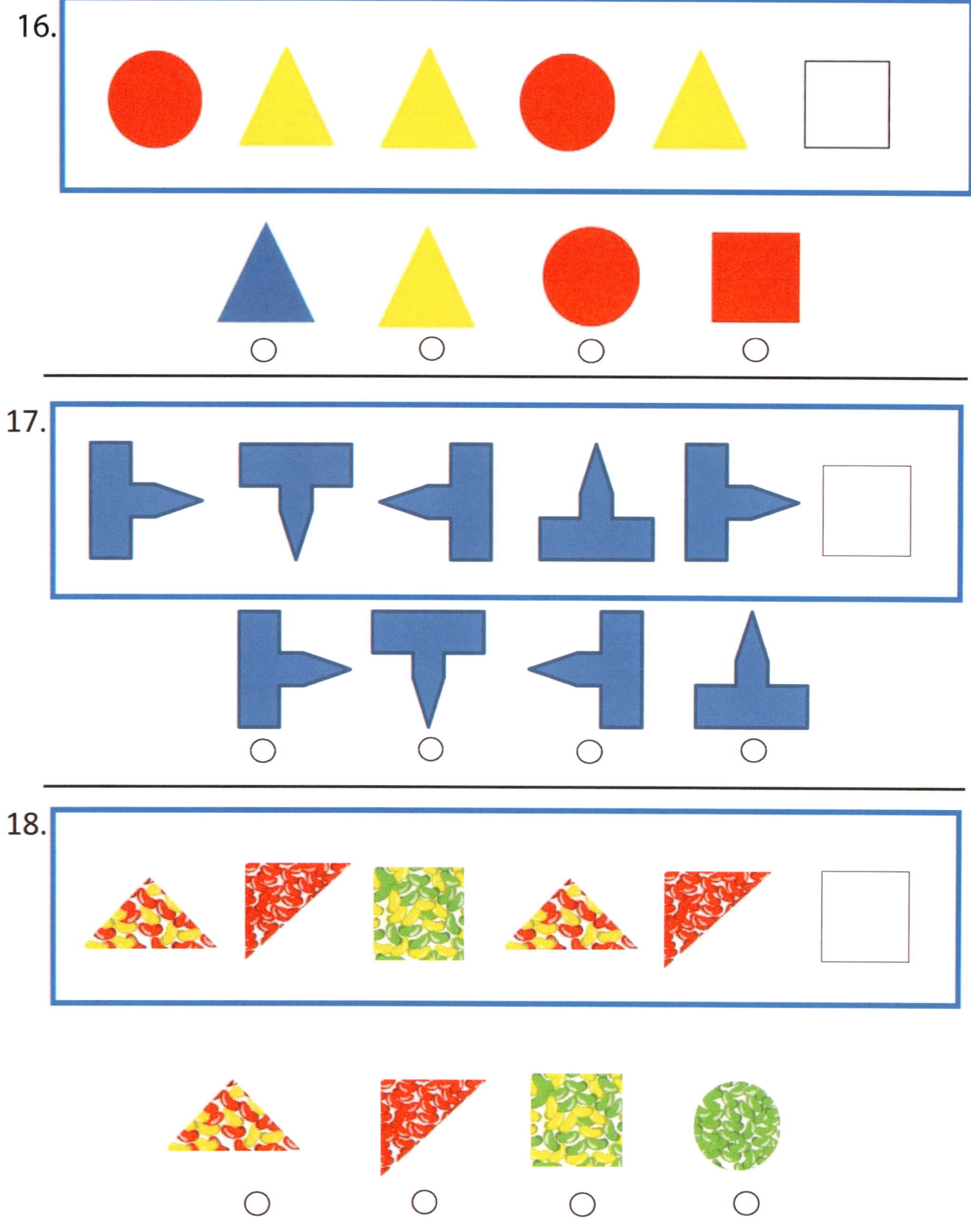

Topic 3   Associations

Draw lines connecting each picture to the most useful tool in that situation.

1.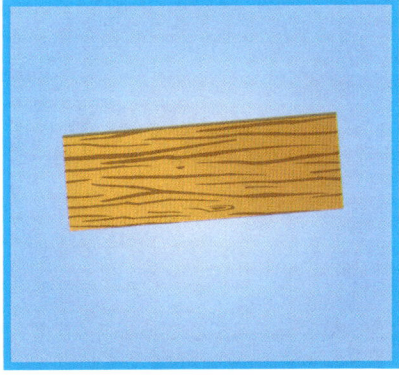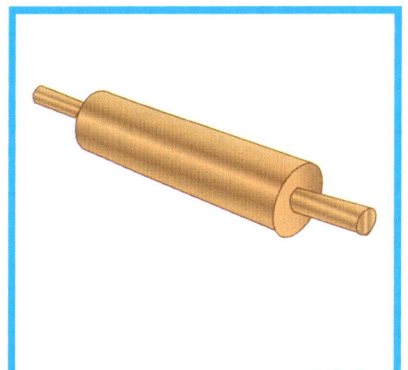

2.

3.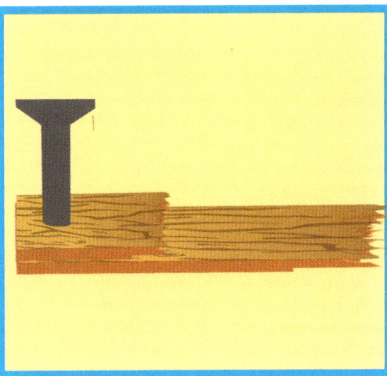

4.

Topic 3   Associations

Draw lines connecting each person to his or her hat.

5.

6.

7.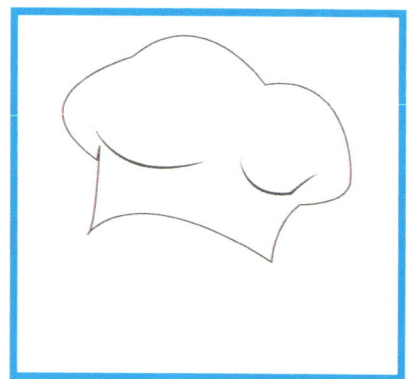

8.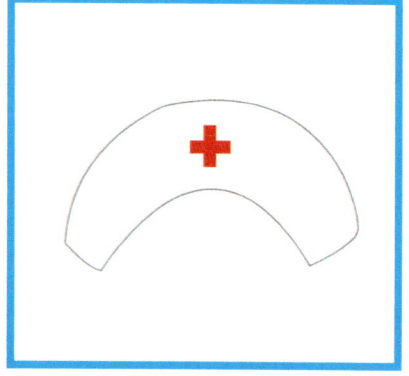

Topic 3							Associations

Draw lines to connect each doll to the clothes he/she is wearing.

9.

10.

11.

12.

Topic 3 Associations

Draw lines to connect each person to the tracks he would make.

13.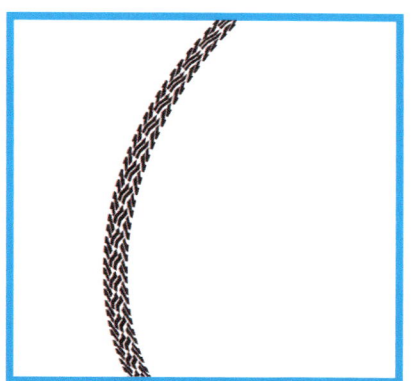

14.

15.

16.

Topic 3   Associations

Draw lines to connect each article of clothing to the pieces it is made up of.

17.

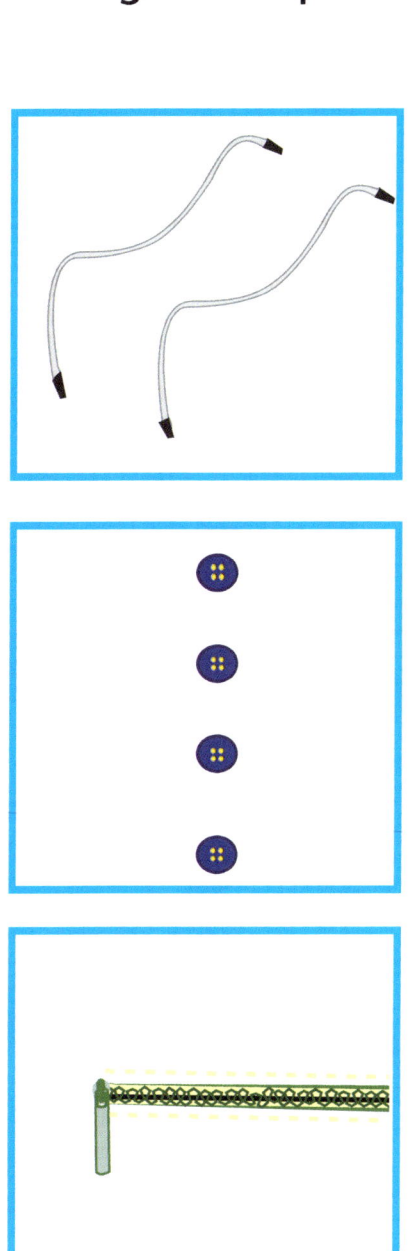

18.

19.

20.

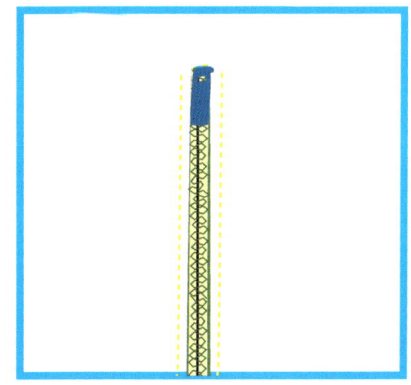

Topic 3   Associations

Draw lines to connect each jellybean carving to the shape it makes.

21.

22.

23.

24.

OLSAT Practice Test

Topic 3   Associations

Draw lines to connect each object with its shadow.

25.

26.

27.

28.

Topic 3　　　　　　　　　　　　　　　　　　　　　　　　　Associations

Draw lines to connect each animal with its footprint.

29. 　　　

30. 　　　

31. 　　　

32. 　　　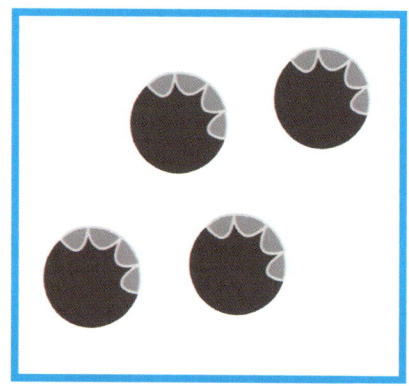

Topic 3   Associations

Draw lines to connect each top to its matching bottom.

33.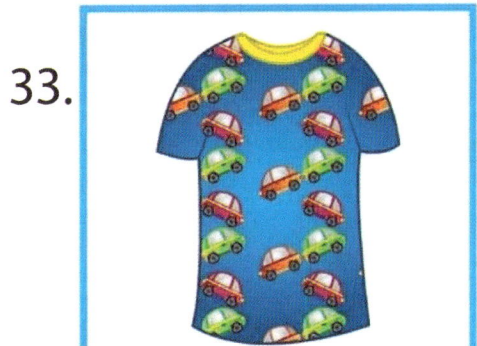

34.

35.

36.

Topic 4 Puzzles

Fill in the circle under the puzzle piece that completes the big picture.

1.

○ ○ ○ ○

2.

○ ○ ○ ○

Topic 4 Puzzles

Draw lines to each scrambled picture to its complete picture.

1.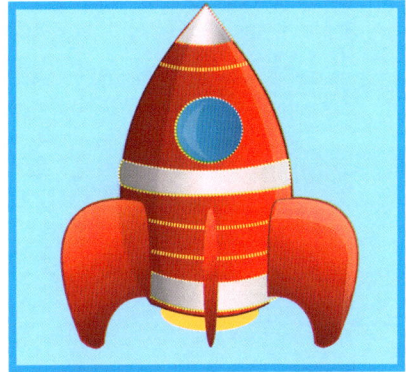

2.

3.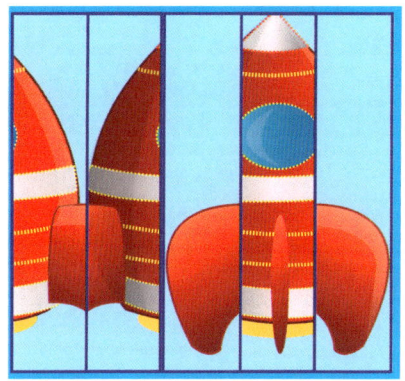

4.

Topic 4 Puzzles

Draw lines to match the puzzle pieces that fit together.

1.

2.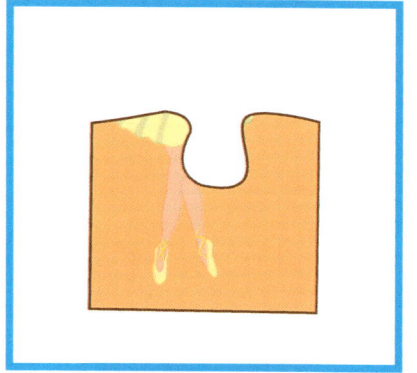

3.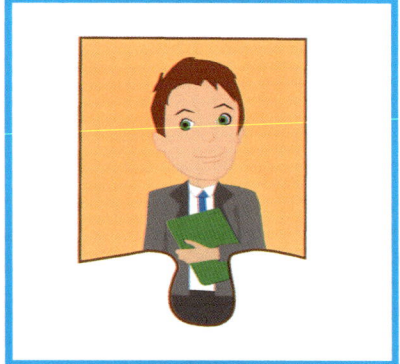

4.

Topic 4   Puzzles

Draw lines to match the puzzle pieces that fit together.

1.

2.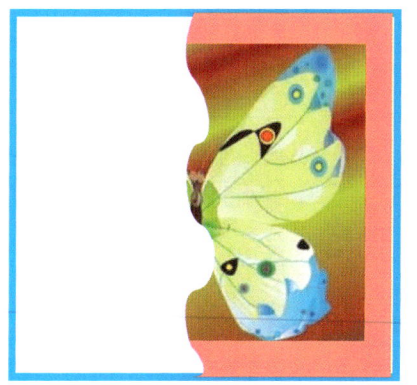

3.

4.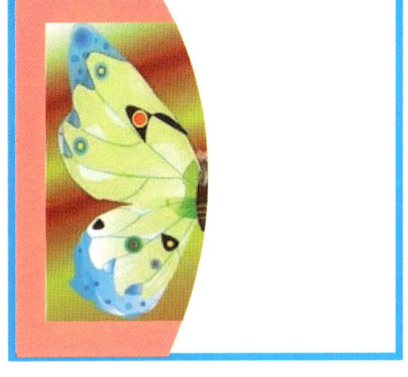

Topic 4 Puzzles

Draw lines to match the blocks that belong together.

1.

2.

3.

4.

Topic 4   Puzzles

Draw lines matching each picture to the piece that best completes it.

1.

2.

3.

4.

Topic 4 Puzzles

Draw lines connecting each picture to the piece that best completes it.

1.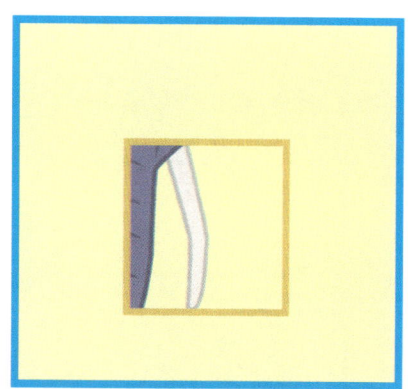

2.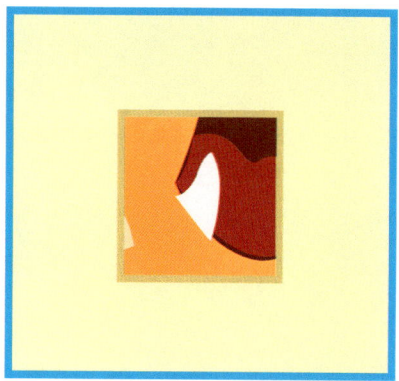

3.

4.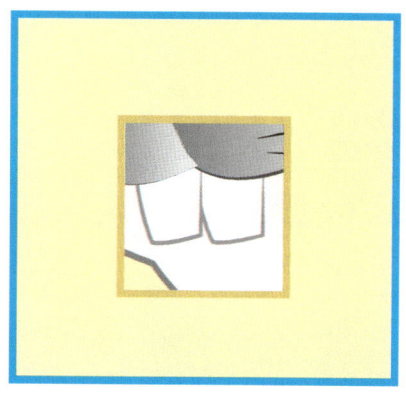

Topic 4　　　　　　　　　　　　　　　　　　　　　　　　Puzzles

Draw lines to connect each animal to its tail.

1. 　　

2. 　　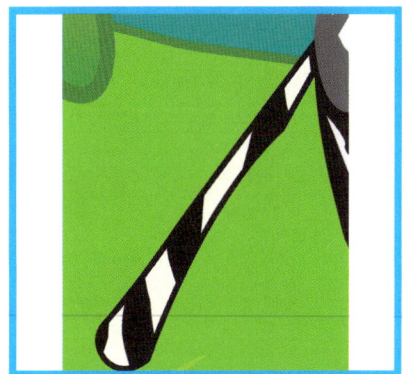

3. 　　

4. 　　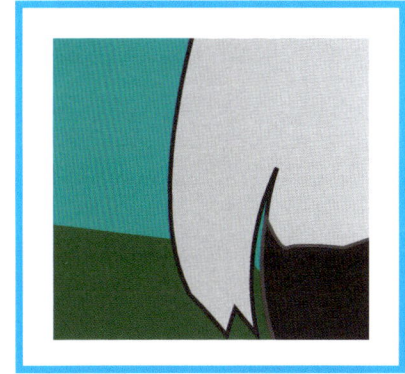

Topic 4 Puzzles

Draw lines to connect each scrambled puzzle to its completed puzzle.

1.

2.

3.

4.

Topic 5 Finding Differences

1. Do you see any differences between the two pictures? Find and circle 4 differences.

Topic 5   Finding Differences

2. Do you see any differences between the two pictures? Find and circle 4 differences.

Topic 5   **Finding Differences**

3. Do you see any differences between the two pictures? Find and circle 4 differences below.

4. Do you see any differences between the two pictures? Find and circle 4 differences below.

Topic 5 — Finding Differences

5. Do you see any differences between the two pictures? Find and circle 4 differences below.

Pi For Kids Inc.©   OLSAT Practice Test

Topic 5 Finding Differences

6. Do you see any differences between the two pictures? Find and circle 4 differences below.

Topic 6 Concentration

Draw lines to connect each animal to its feet.

1.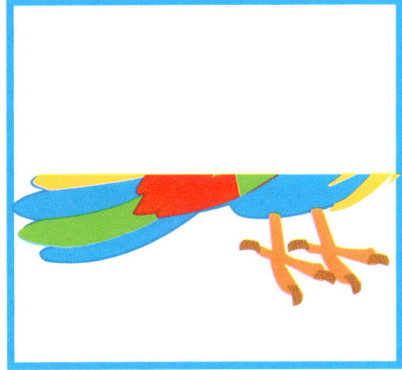

2.

3.

4.

Topic 6   Concentration

Draw lines to match pictures from the left and right that fit together.

1.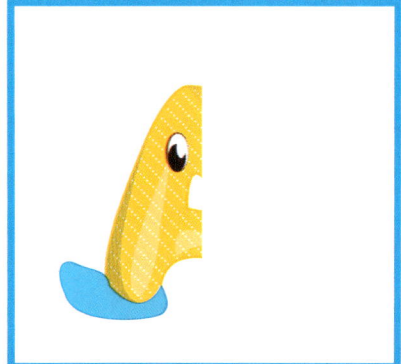

2.

3.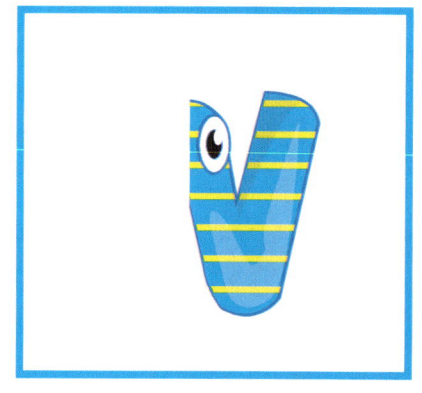

4.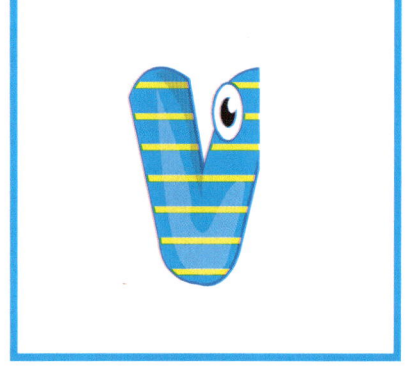

Topic 6 — Concentration

Draw lines to connect each close-up to its bigger picture.

1.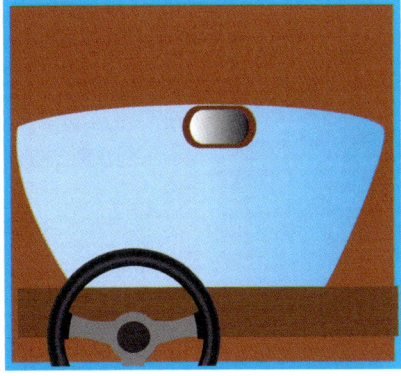
2.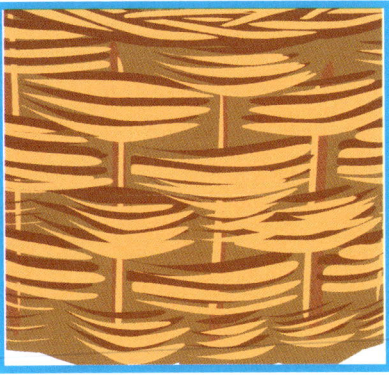
3.
4.

Topic 6 Concentration

Draw lines to connect each person to his/her shoes.

1.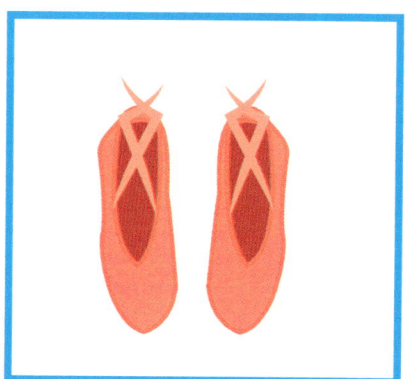

2.

3.

4.

Topic 6　　　　　　　　　　　　　　　　　　　　　　　Concentration

Draw lines to connect each animal to its body parts.

1.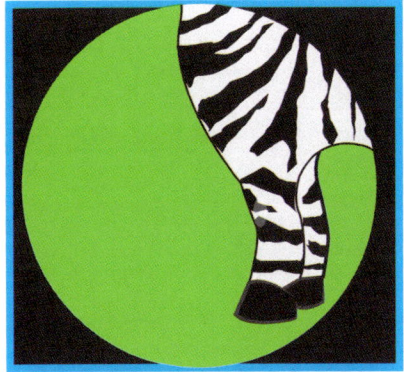

2.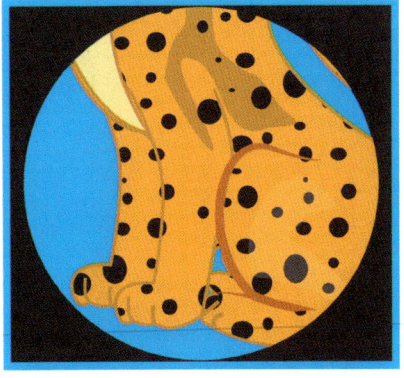

3.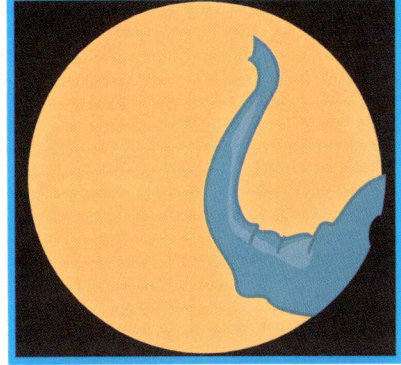

4.

Topic 6 Concentration

Draw lines to connect each container to its lid.

1.

2.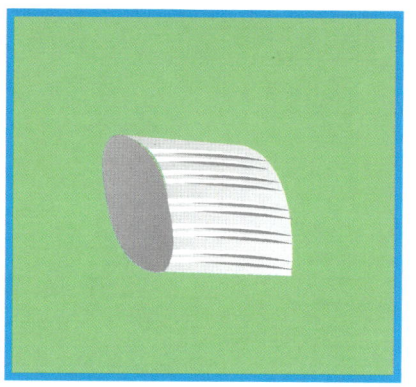

3.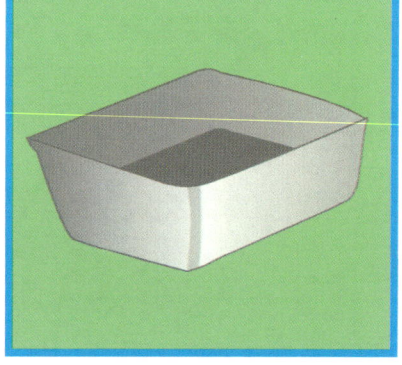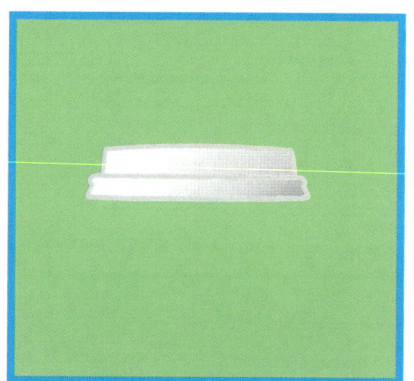

4.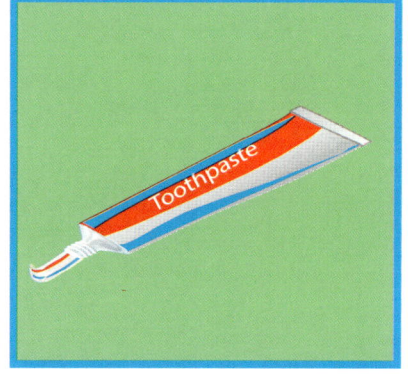

Topic 6   Concentration

Draw lines to connect each person or object on the right to the place where you would find it.

1.

2.

3.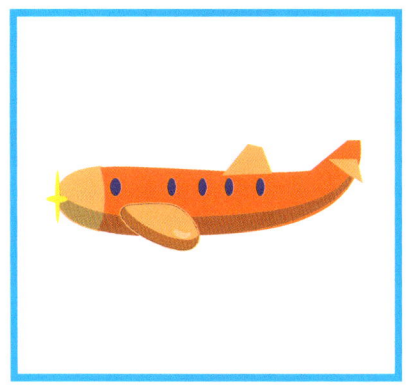

4.

Topic 6   Concentration

Draw lines to connect each box to the object that would fit best inside.

1.

2.

3.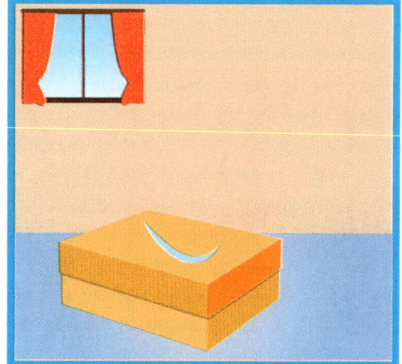

4.

Topic 6 Concentration

Draw lines to connect the toy in each picture on the left to its parts shown on the right.

1.

2.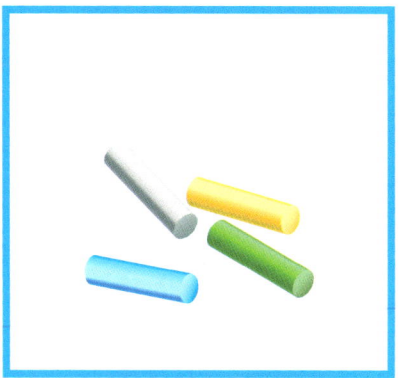

3.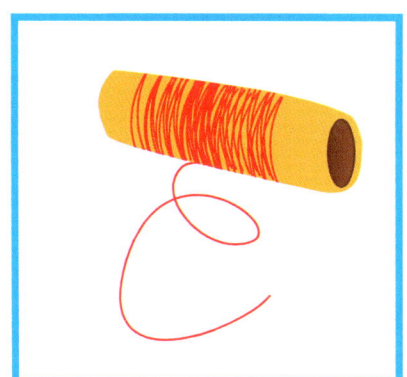

4.

Topic 6 Concentration

Draw lines to connect each cookie cutter to the cookies it would be able to make.

1.

2.

3.

4.

Topic 7 Picture Analogies

Fill in the circle under the picture that belongs in the empty box so that each row has the same relationship.

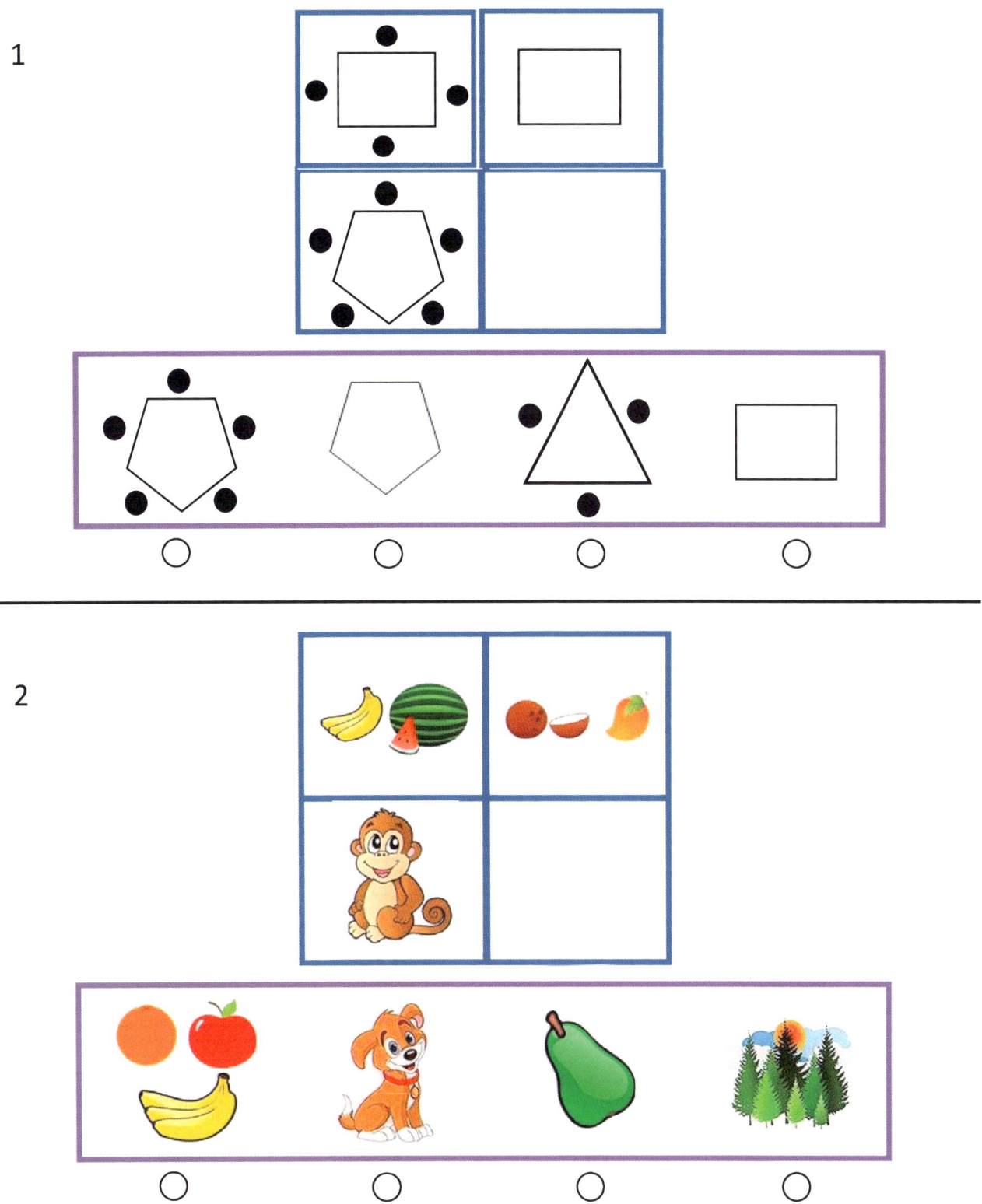

1

2

Pi For Kids Inc.© OLSAT Practice Test 49

Topic 7   Picture Analogies

Fill in the circle under the picture that belongs in the empty box so that each row has the same relationship.

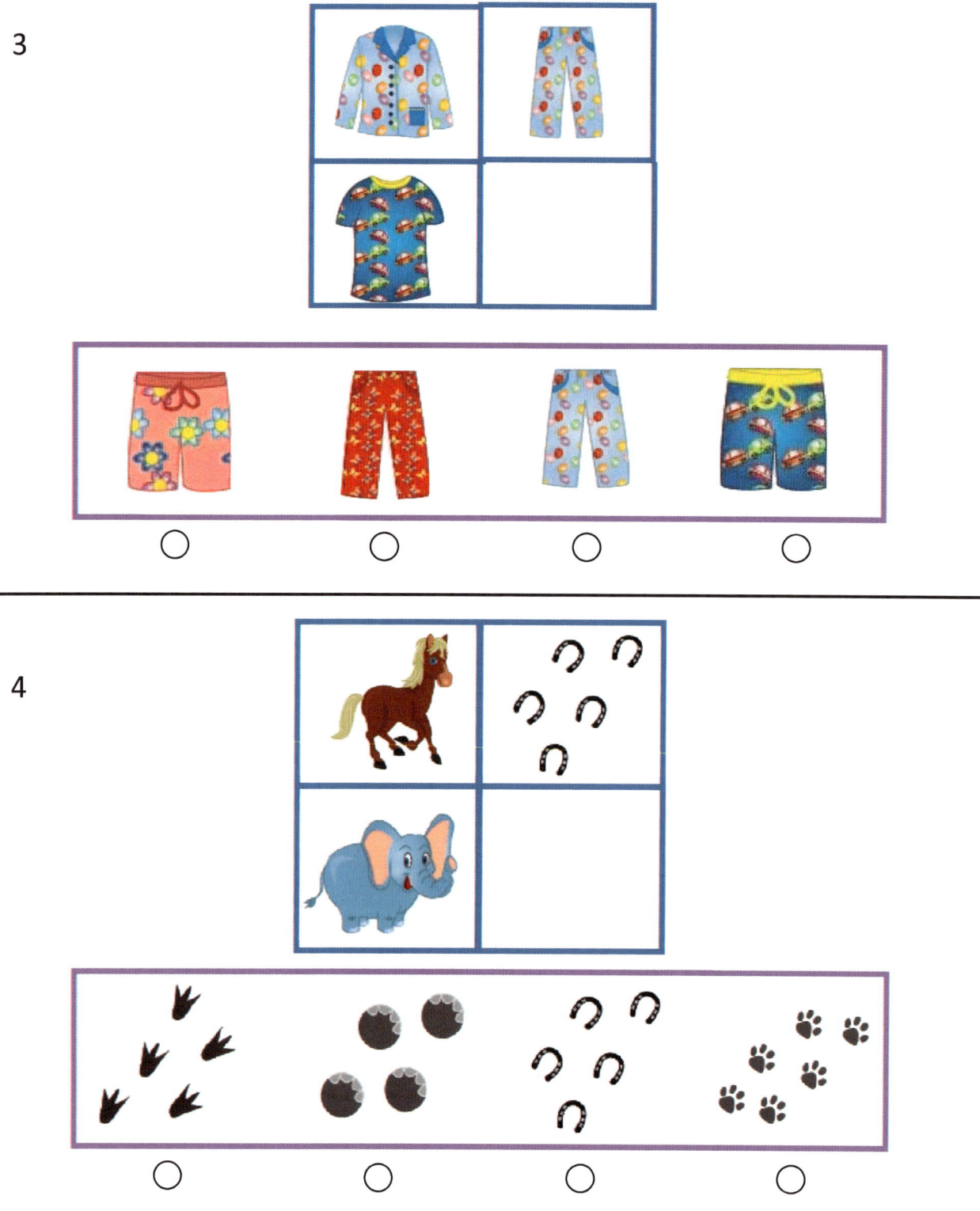

Topic 7　　　　　　　　　　　　　　　　　　　　　Picture Analogies

Fill in the circle under the picture that belongs in the empty box so that each row has the same relationship.

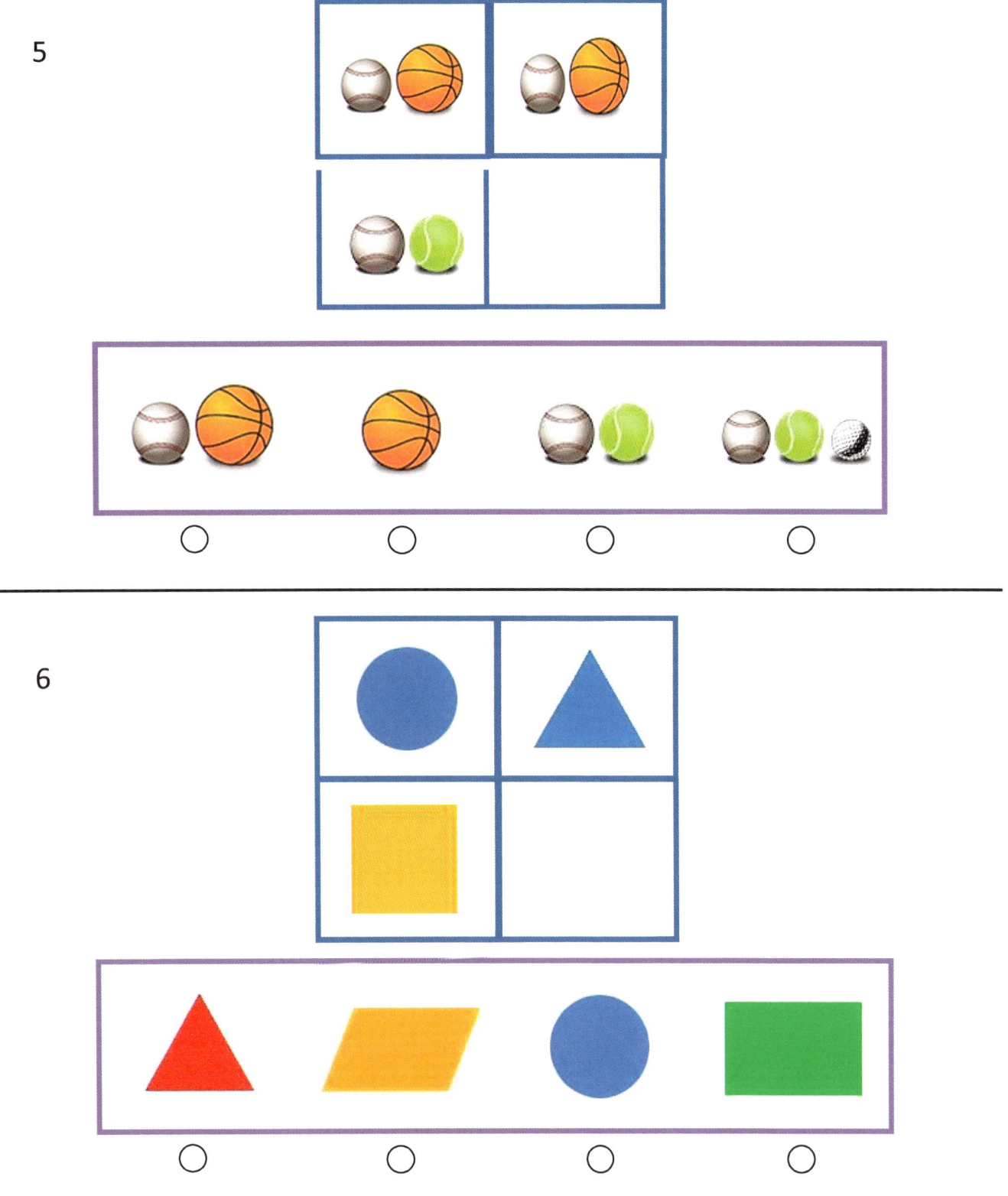

Topic 7 Picture Analogies

Fill in the circle under the picture that belongs in the empty box so that each row has the same relationship.

7

8

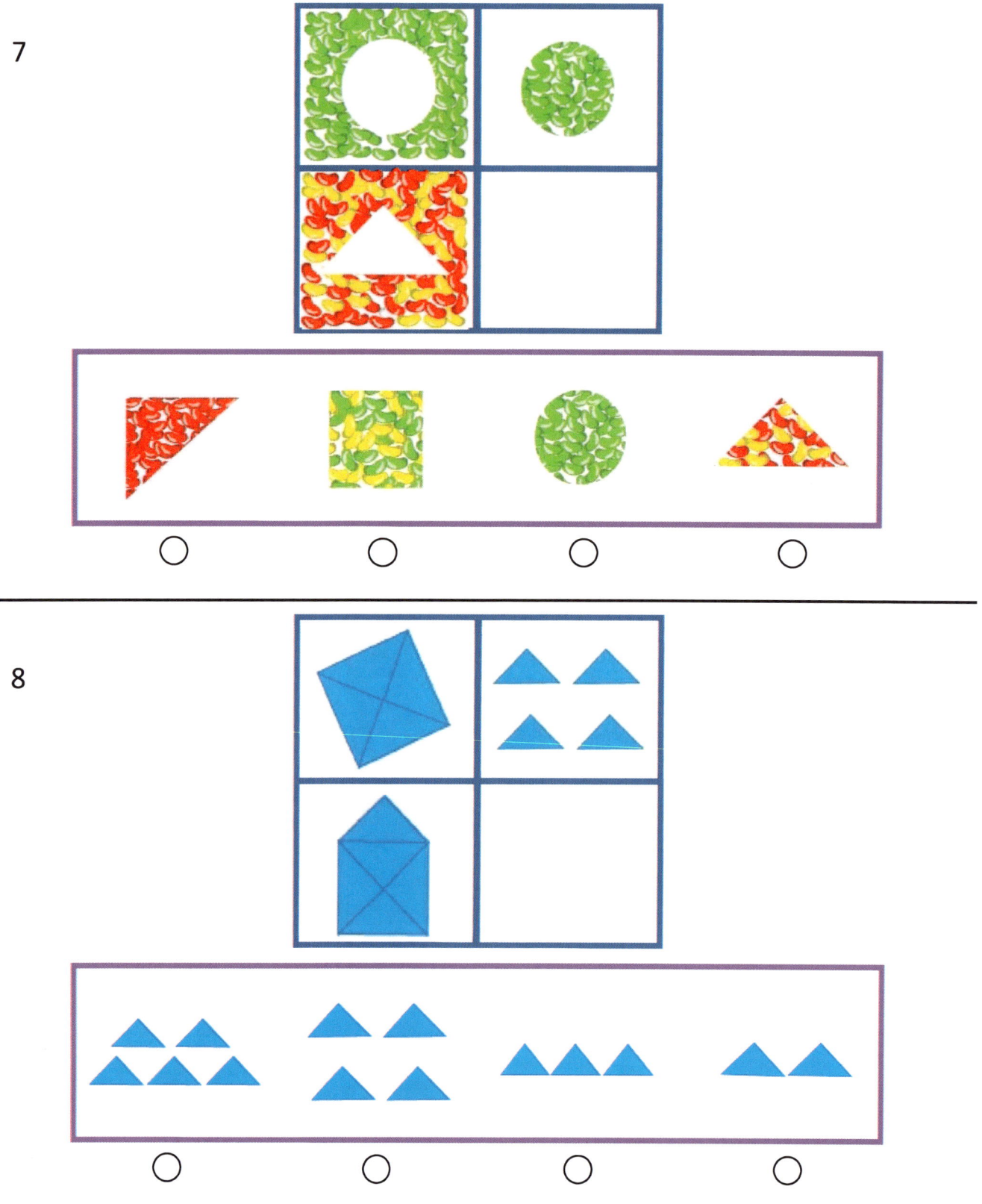

52 OLSAT Practice Test Pi For Kids Inc.©

Topic 7 Picture Analogies

Fill in the circle under the picture that belongs in the empty box so that each row has the same relationship.

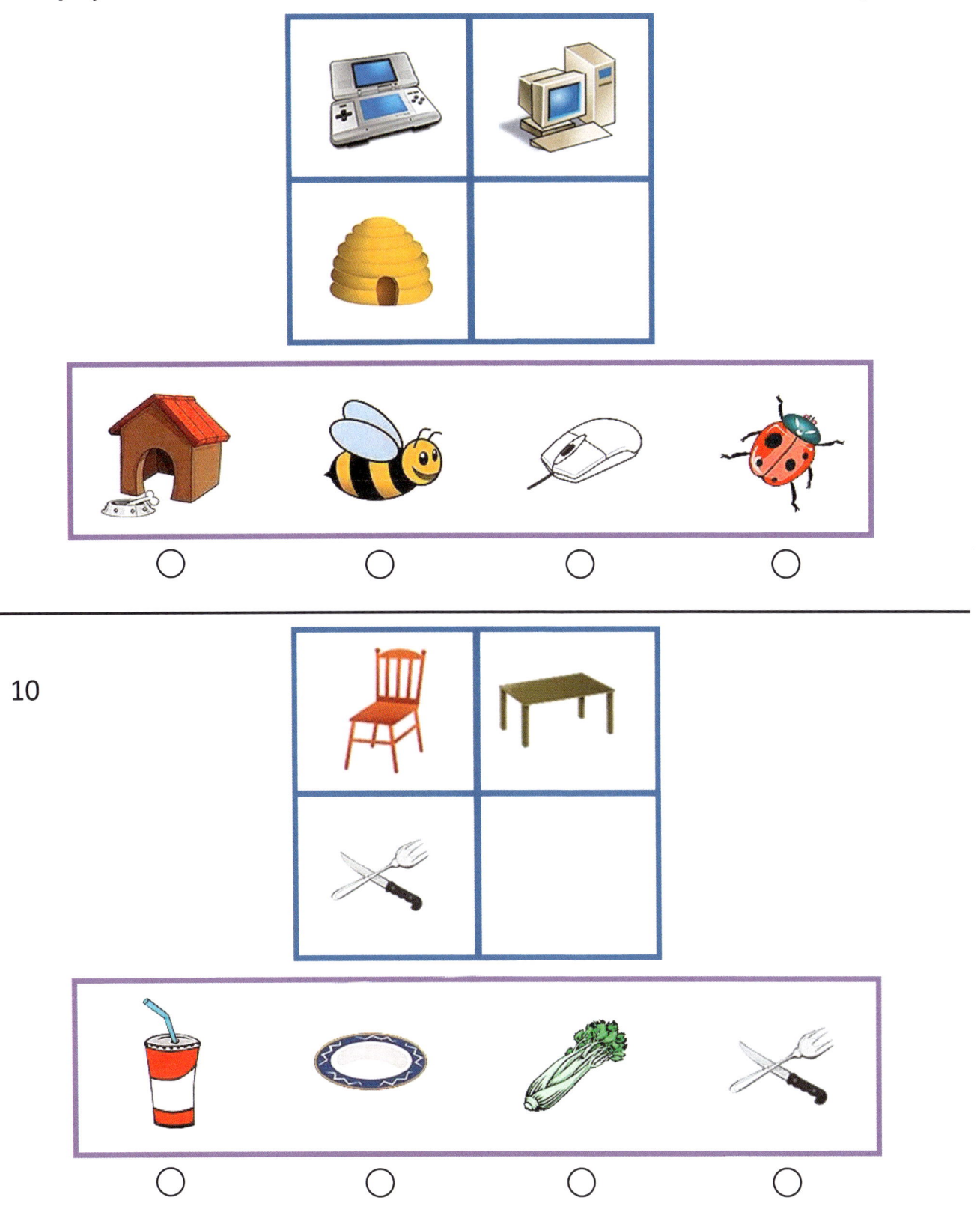

10

OLSAT Practice Test

Topic 7   Picture Analogies

Fill in the circle under the picture that belongs in the empty box so that each row has the same relationship.

11

12

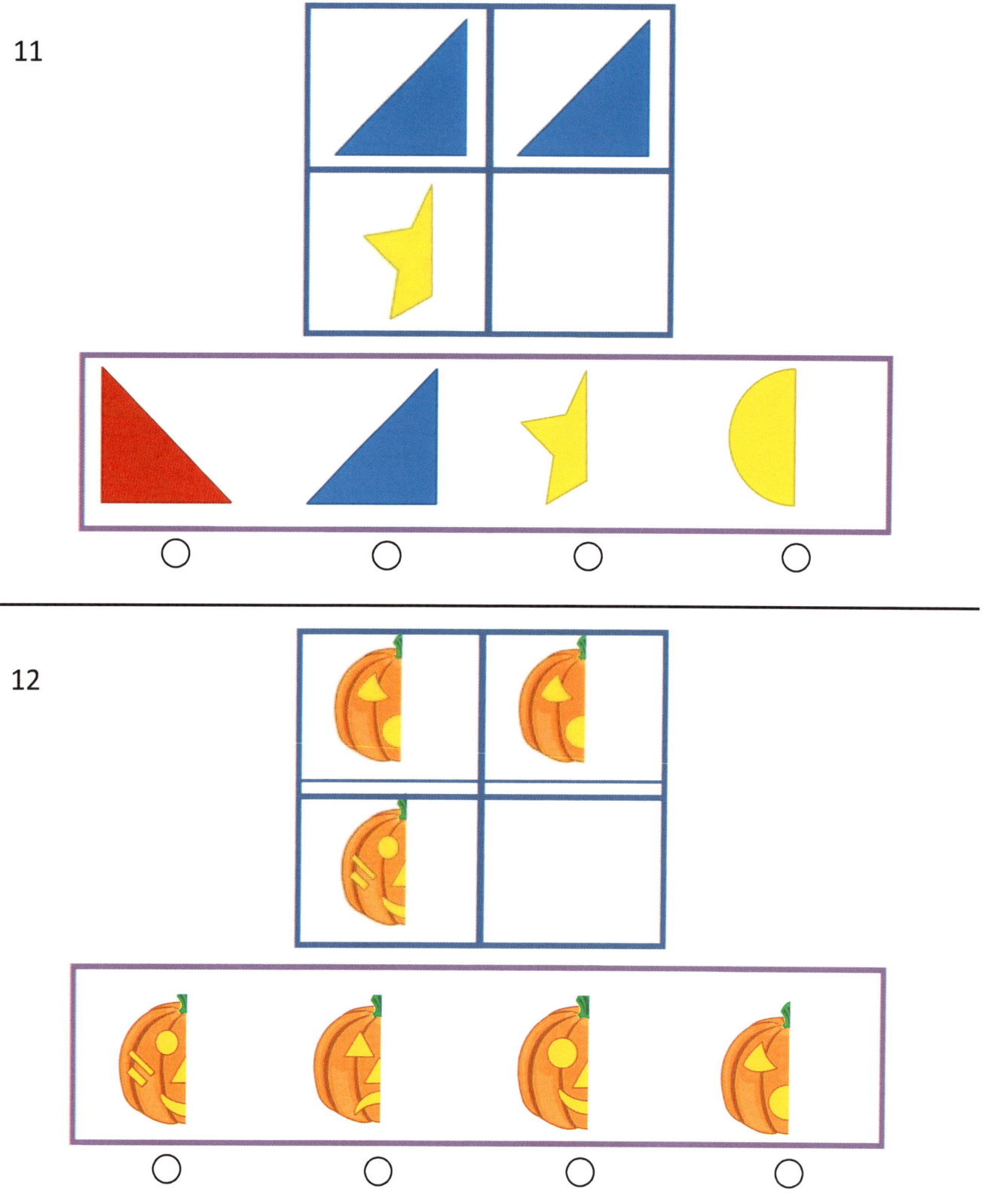

OLSAT Practice Test

Topic 7 Picture Analogies

Fill in the circle under the picture that belongs in the empty box so that each row has the same relationship.

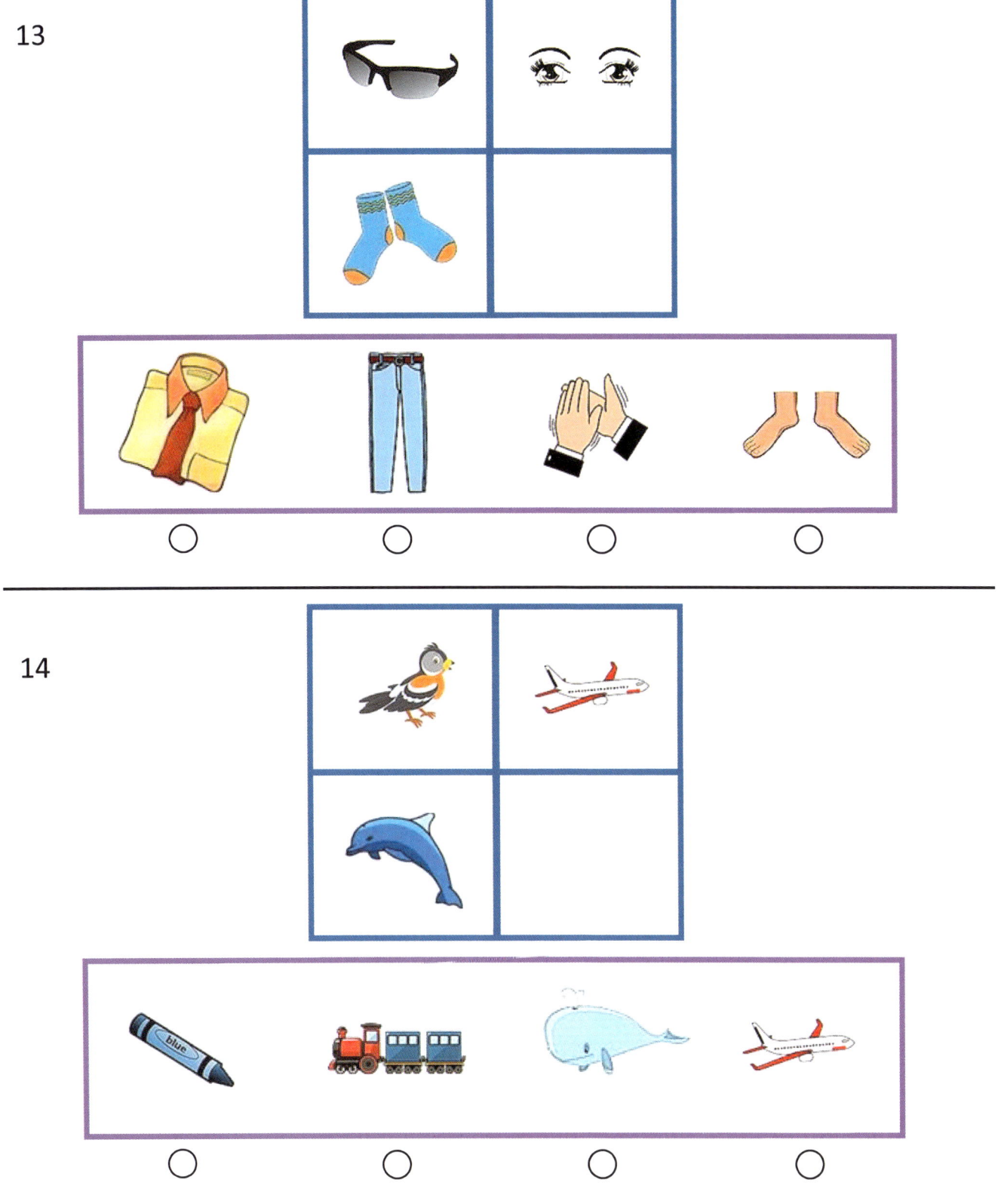

Topic 7 Picture Analogies

Fill in the circle under the picture that belongs in the empty box so that each row has the same relationship.

15

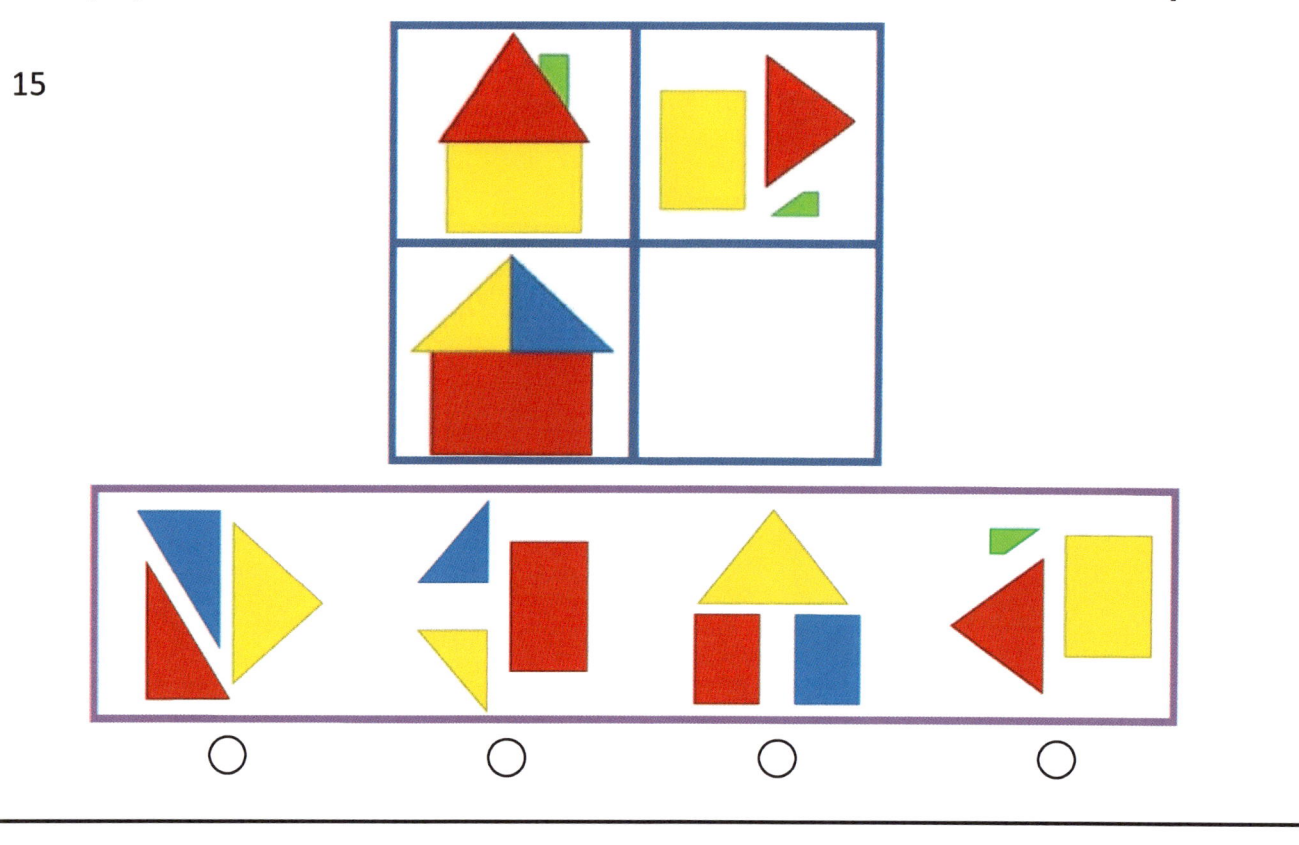

16

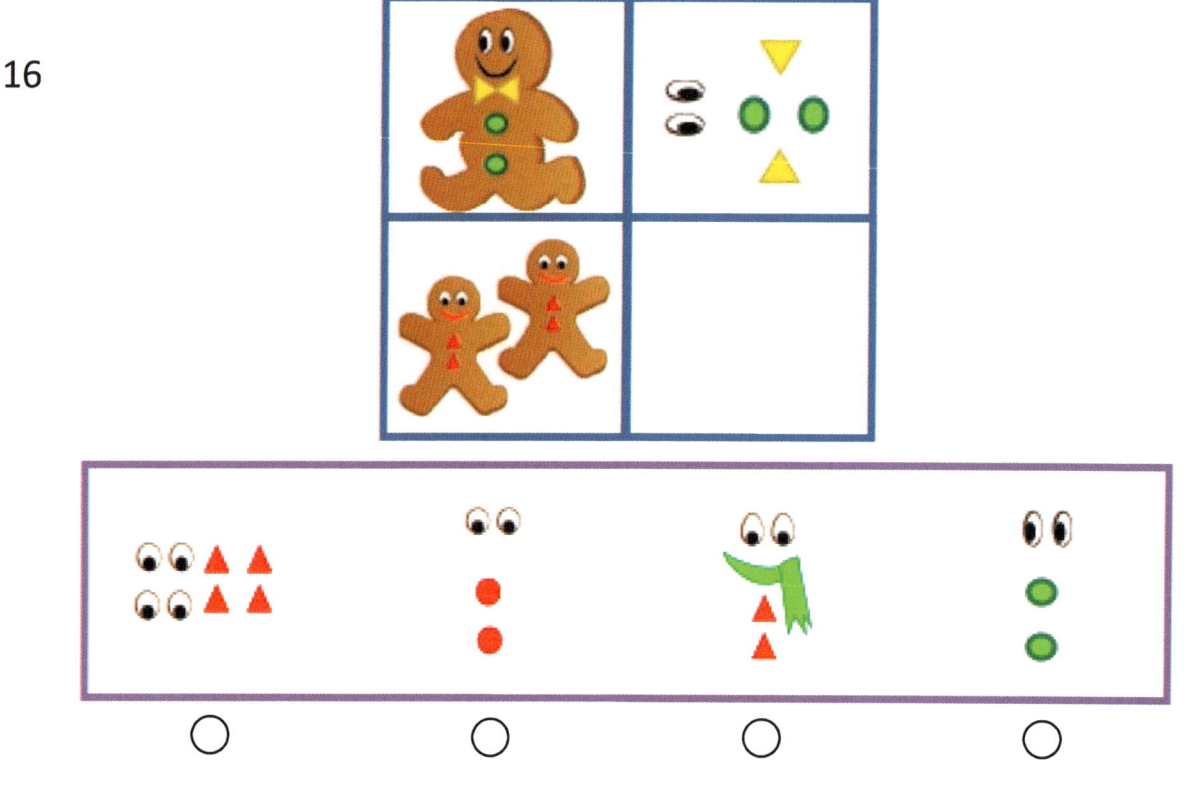

OLSAT Practice Test

Topic 7   Picture Analogies

Fill in the circle under the picture that belongs in the empty box so that each row has the same relationship.

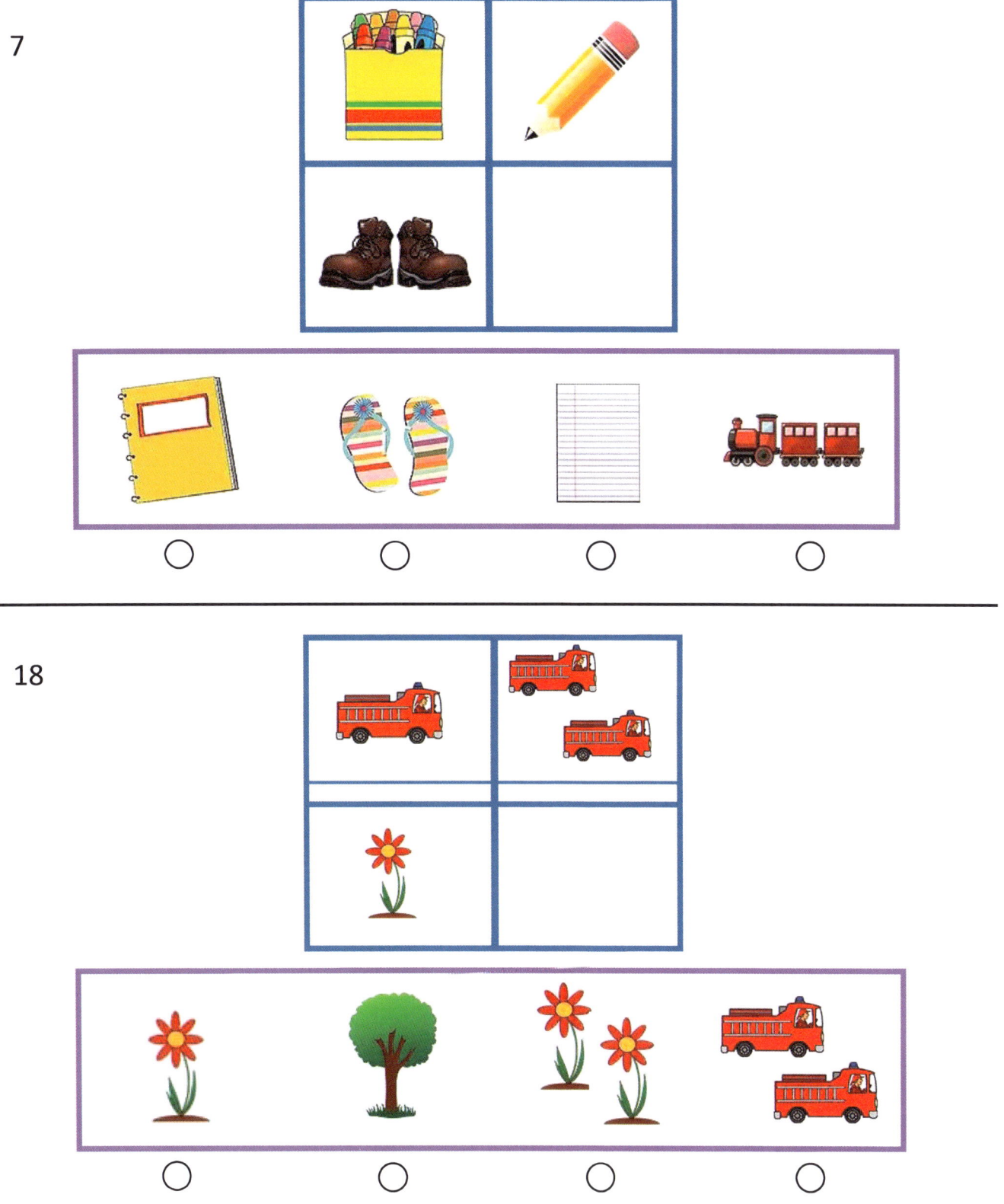

Topic 7   Picture Analogies

Fill in the circle under the picture that belongs in the empty box so that each row has the same relationship.

19

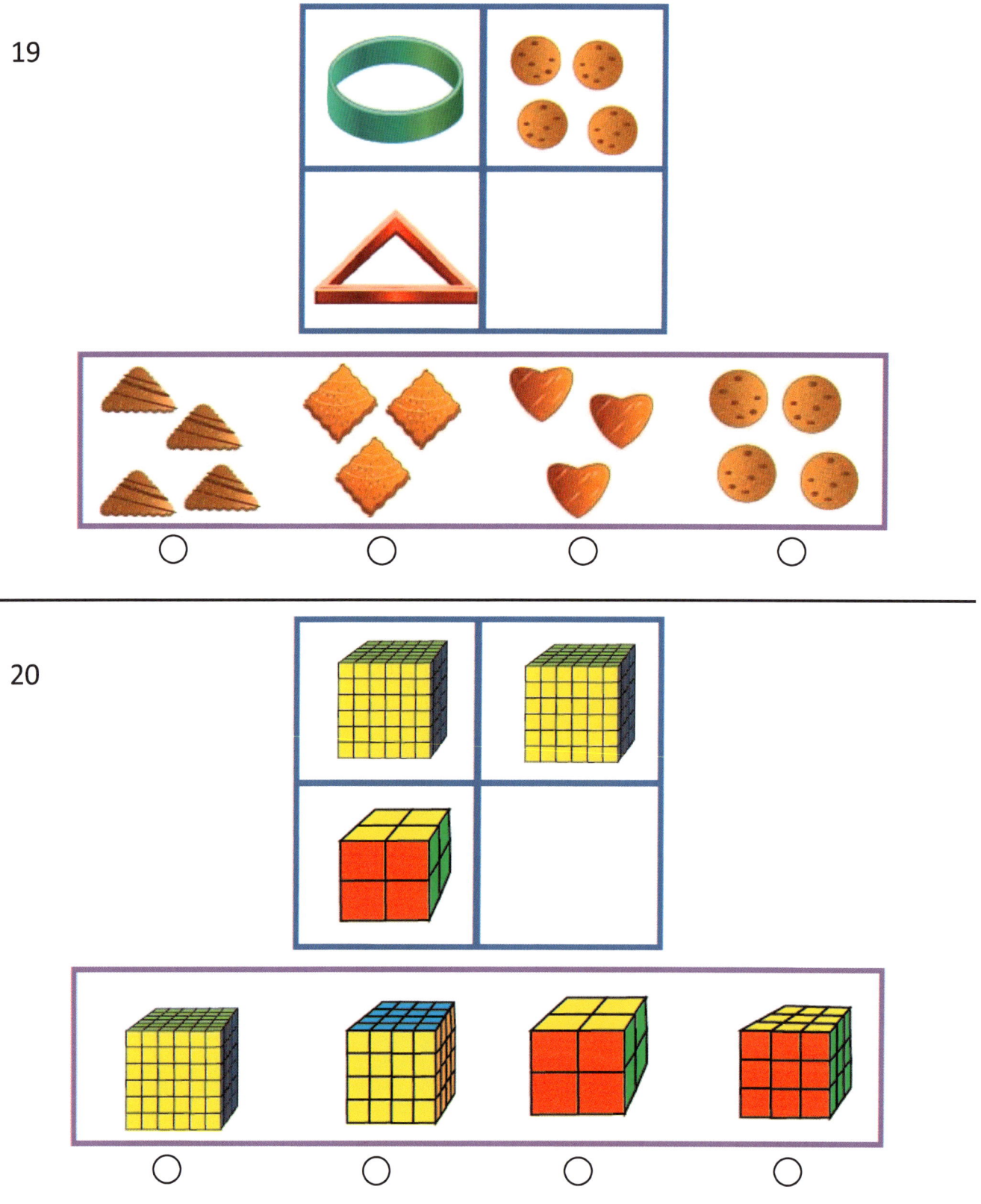

20

Topic 7   Picture Analogies

Fill in the circle under the picture that belongs in the empty box so that each row has the same relationship.

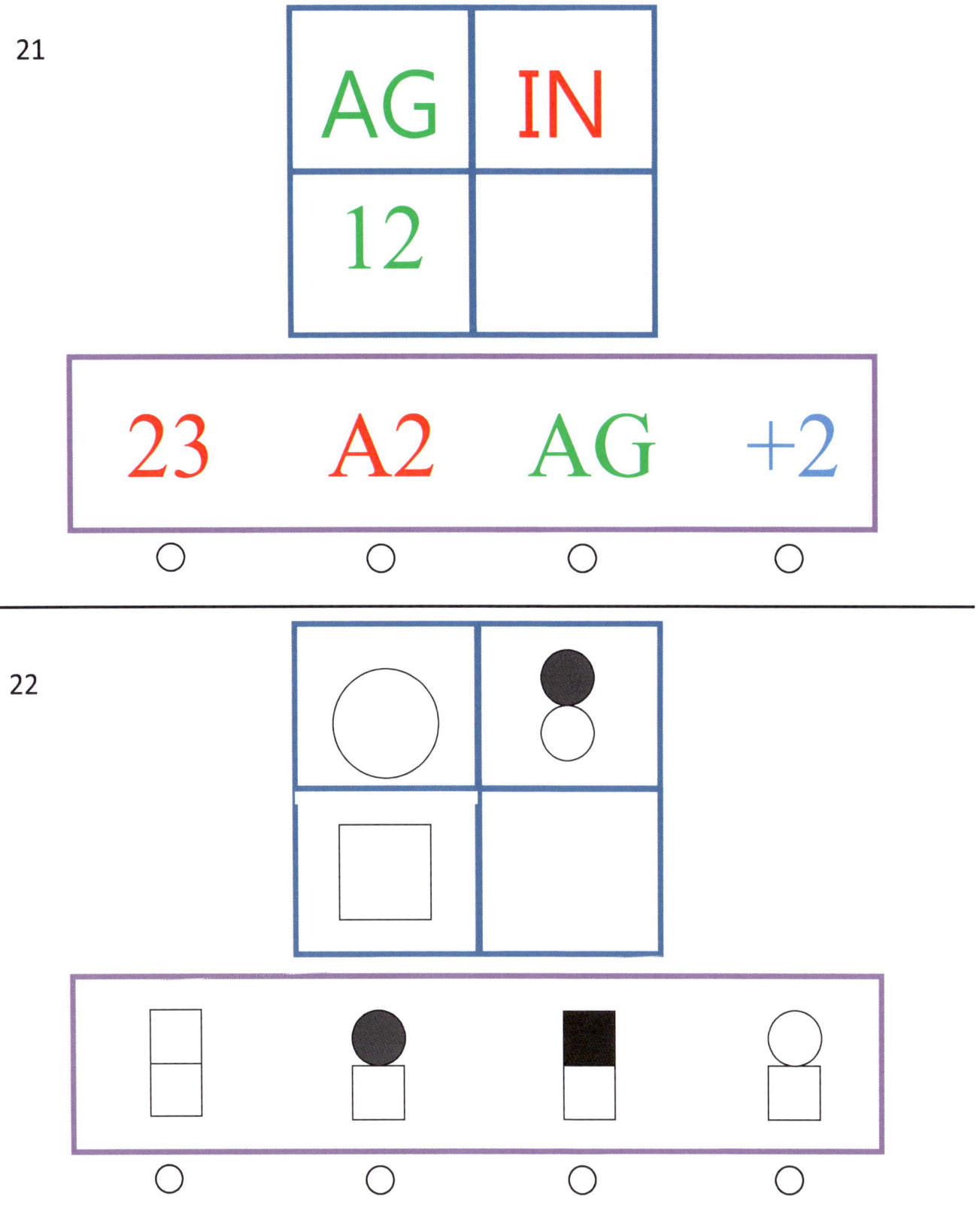

Topic 8 Visual Skills

Draw lines to connect the same fruits.

1.

2.

3.

4.

Topic 8　　　　　　　　　　　　　　　　　　　　　　　　　Visual Skills

Draw lines to connect each store to the objects that you could buy inside.

1. 　　

2. 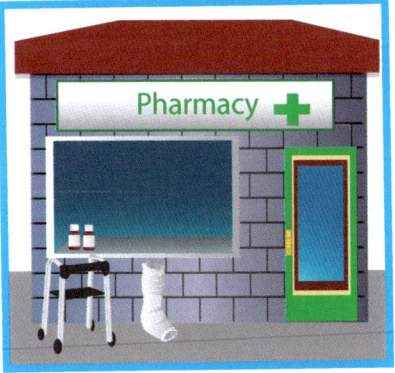　　

3. 　　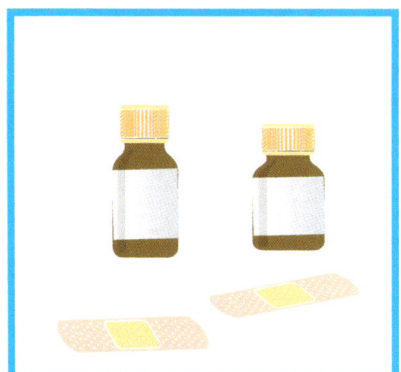

4. 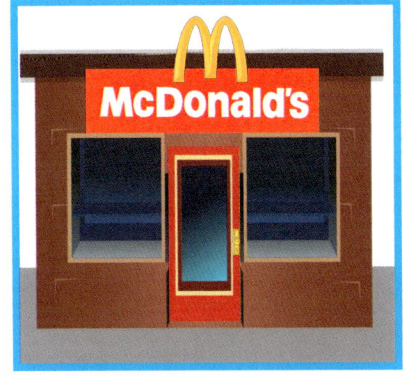　　

Topic 8   Visual Skills

Draw lines to each person's back view to their front view.

1.

2.

3.

4.

Topic 8   Visual Skills

Draw lines to each fruit to its skin.

1.

2.

3.

4.

Topic 8 Visual Skills

Draw lines to connect each object to its top view (bird's eye view).

1.

2.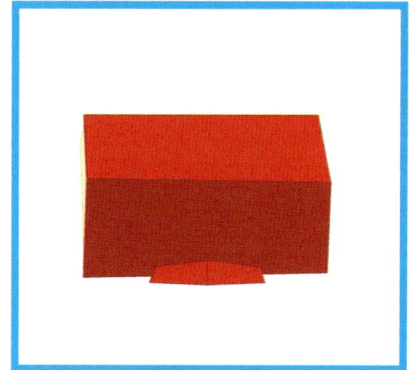

3.

4.

Topic 8 — Visual Skills

Draw lines to connect each mosaic to the object or person that it is showing.

1.

2.

3.

4.

Pi For Kids Inc.©   OLSAT Practice Test

Topic 8 　　　　　　　　　　　　　　　　　　　　　　　　　Visual Skills

Draw lines to connect each pair of club members to their correct club T-shirts.

1.

2.

3.

4.

Topic 8 Visual Skills

Draw lines to connect each garden to its corresponding pots of plants.

1.

2.

3.

4.

Topic 9   Critical Thinking

Draw lines to connect each plate to its matching bowl.

1.

2.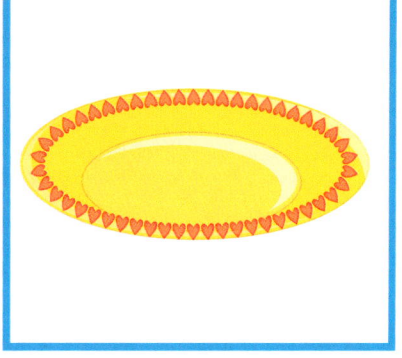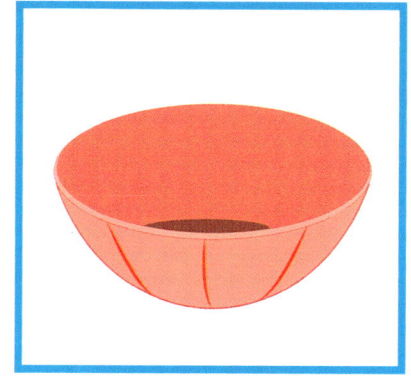

3.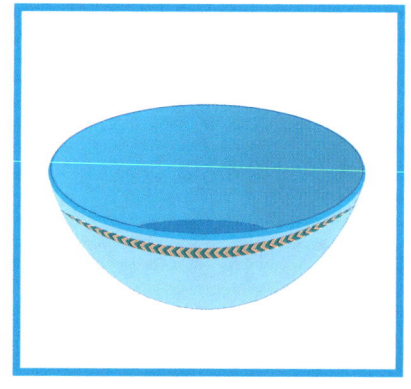

4.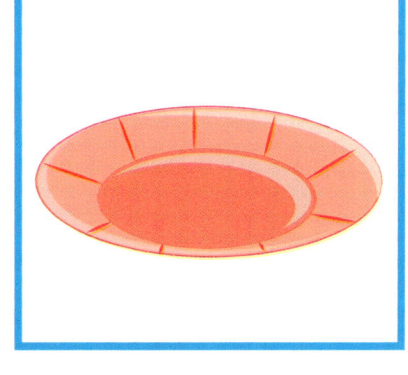

Topic 9   Critical Thinking

Draw lines to connect each picture on the left to the object(s) on the right that are best associated with it.

5.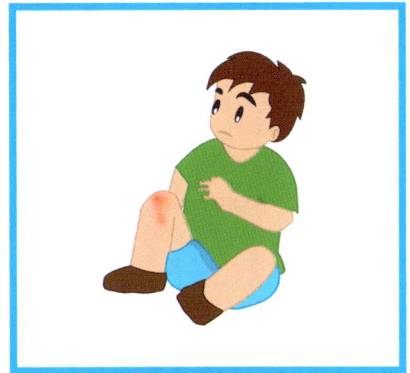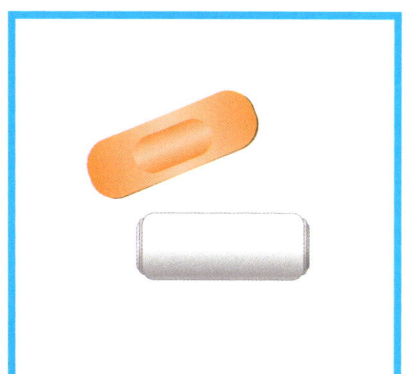

6.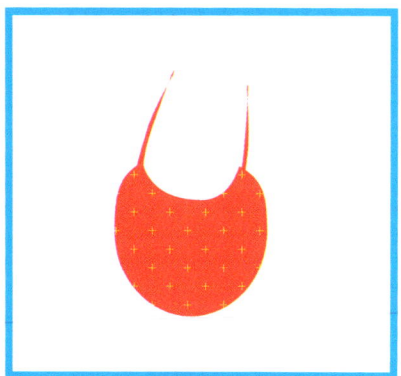

7.

8.

Topic 9 Critical Thinking

Draw lines to connect the people on the left with a picture on the right that is most suited for them.

9.

10.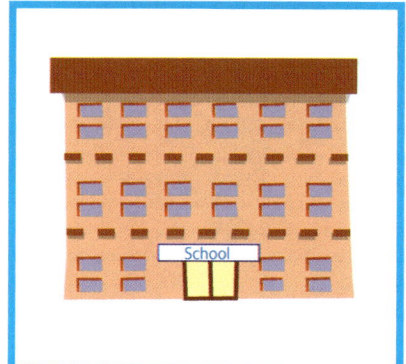

11.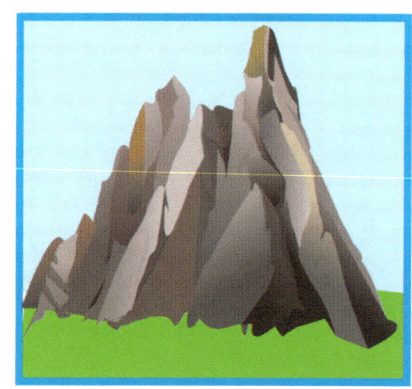

12.

Topic 9   Critical Thinking

Draw lines to connect pictures that show the same season.

13.

14.

15.

16.

Topic 9 Critical Thinking

Draw lines to connect each person to his/her appropriate vehicle.

17.

18.

19.

20.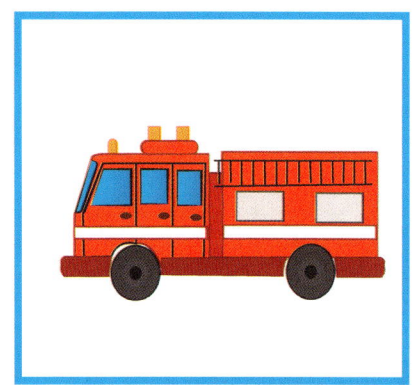

OLSAT Practice Test

Topic 9 — Critical Thinking

Draw lines to connect pictures that are most likely taking place at the same event or time.

21.

22.

23.

24.

Topic 10 Sequences

Write the numbers 1, 2, 3, or 4 in each of the little white boxes below to show the order that the pictures belong in.

1.

74 OLSAT Practice Test Pi For Kids Inc.©

Topic 10   Sequences

Write the numbers 1, 2, 3, or 4 in each of the little white boxes below to show the order that the pictures belong in.

2.

Topic 10   Sequences

Write the numbers 1, 2, 3, or 4 in each of the little white boxes below to show the order that the pictures belong in.

3.

OLSAT Practice Test

Topic 10 Sequences

Write the numbers 1, 2, 3, or 4 in each of the little white boxes below to show the order that the pictures belong in.

4.

Pi For Kids Inc.© OLSAT Practice Test 77

Topic 10 Sequences

Write the numbers 1, 2, 3, or 4 in each of the little white boxes below to show the order that the pictures belong in.

5.

Topic 10 Sequences

Write the numbers 1, 2, 3, or 4 in each of the little white boxes below to show the order that the pictures belong in.

6.

Topic 10   Sequences

Write the numbers 1, 2, 3, or 4 in each of the little white boxes below to show the order that the pictures belong in.

7.

Topic 11 Math Concept

Draw lines to connect each vehicle to the correct number of wheels it should have.

1.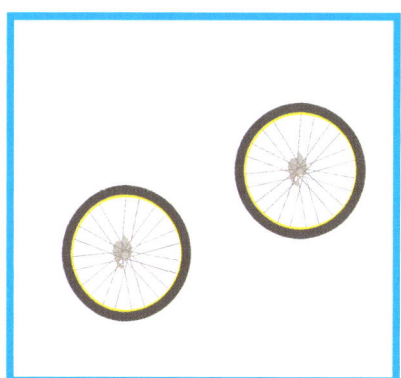

2.

3.

4.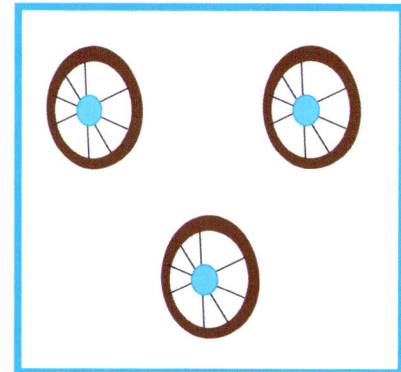

Topic 11   Math Concept

Draw lines to connect each group of people to the total number of chairs that they would need to sit down.

5.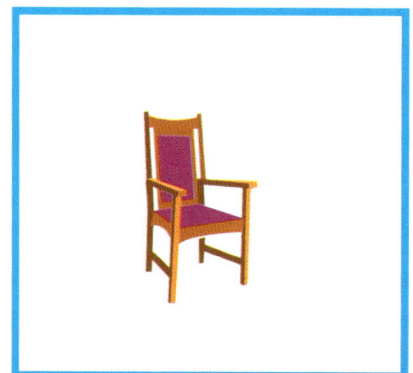

6.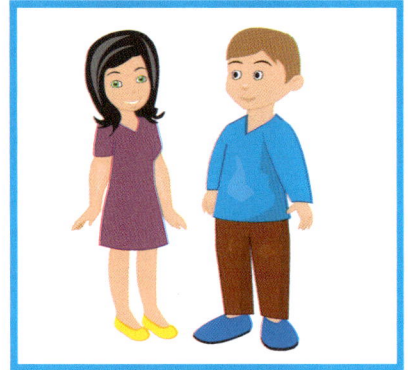

7.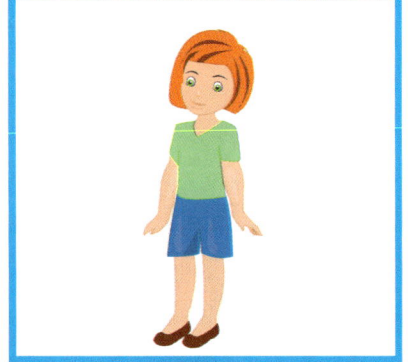

8.

Topic 11　　　　　　　　　　　　　　　　　　　　　　　　　　　Math Concept

Draw lines to connect each numbered dice to show the total number of people or objects in each picture.

9. 　　

10. 　　

11. 　　

12. 　　

Topic 11 Math Concepts

Draw lines to connect pictures from the left and right that show the same number of objects.

13.

14.

15.

16.

Topic 11	Math Concepts

Draw lines to connect each pair of die to a picture showing that total number of objects.

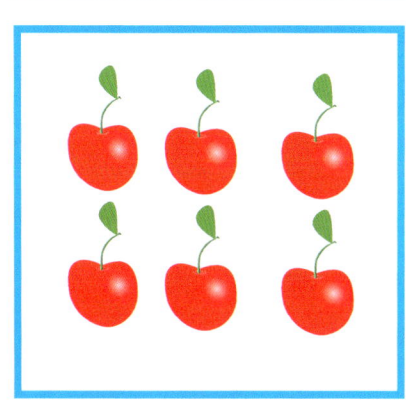

Topic 11 Math Concept

Draw lines to connect pictures to show the total number of objects left after some are taken away.

21.

22.

23.

24.

Topic 11   Math Concept

Draw lines to connect pictures to show the number of birds that are left after some fly away.

25.

26.

27.

28.

NNAT2 Additional Practice

Often, the OLSAT and the NNAT is tested as a whole to younger children. The NNAT, a nonverbal test, is a valid assessment of children's ability to complete patterns, reason using analogies, and visualize combined objects, regardless of their primary language. On the other hand, the OLSAT is a verbal test that measures children's ability to follow directions and solve arithmetic problems through verbal instruction in English.

The NNAT2 is divided into 4 sections as follows:
1. Pattern Completion
2. Reasoning by Analogy
3. Serial Reasoning
4. Spatial Visualization

NNAT Additional Practice

1

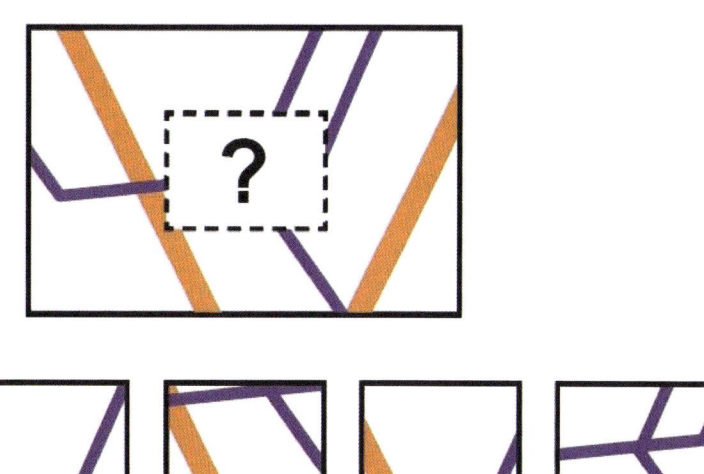

2

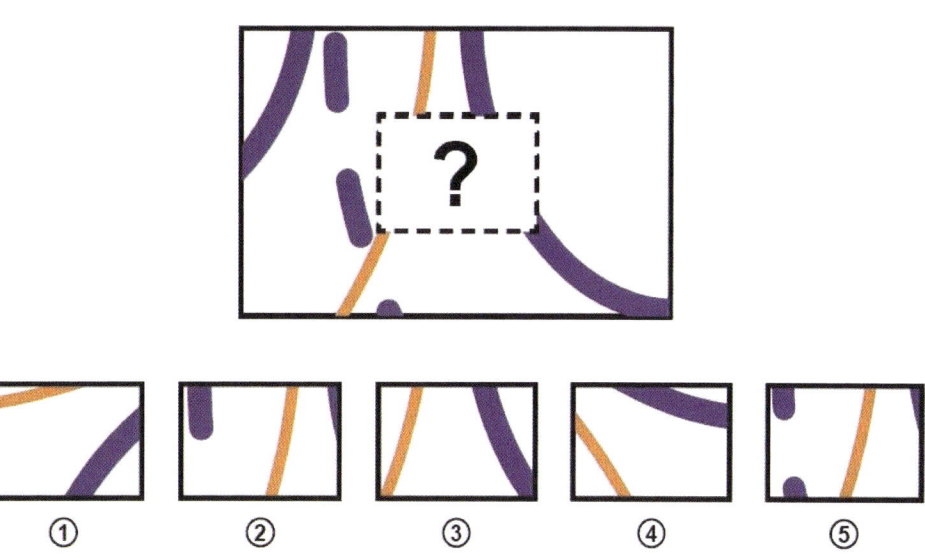

Pi For Kids Inc.©   OLSAT Practice Test   89

3

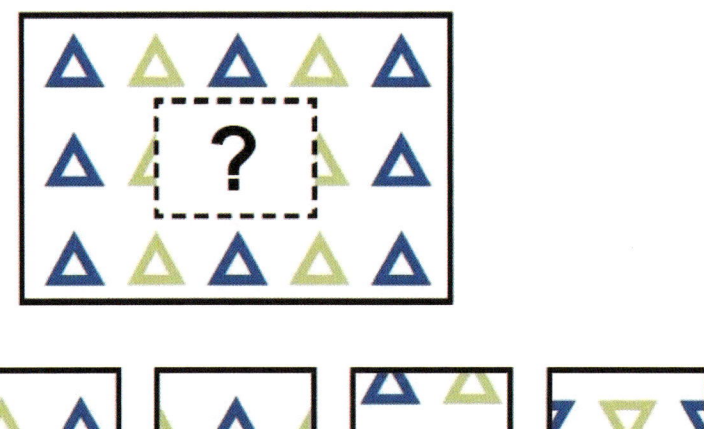

4

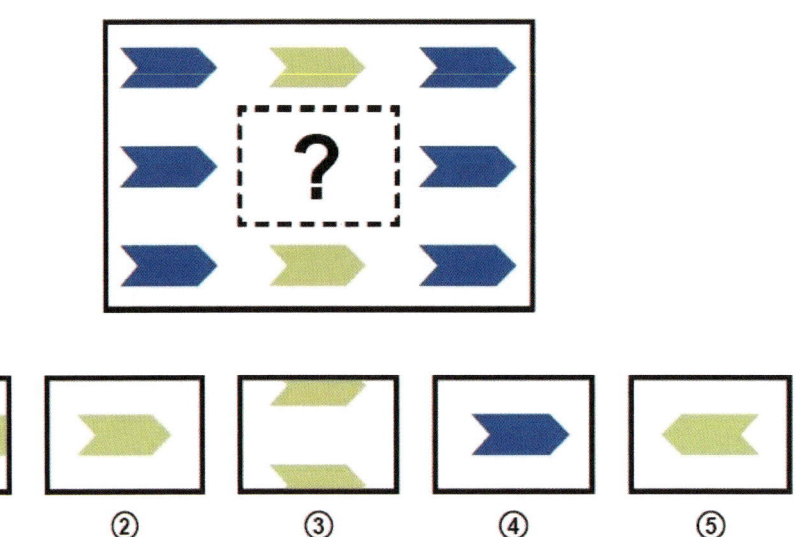

5

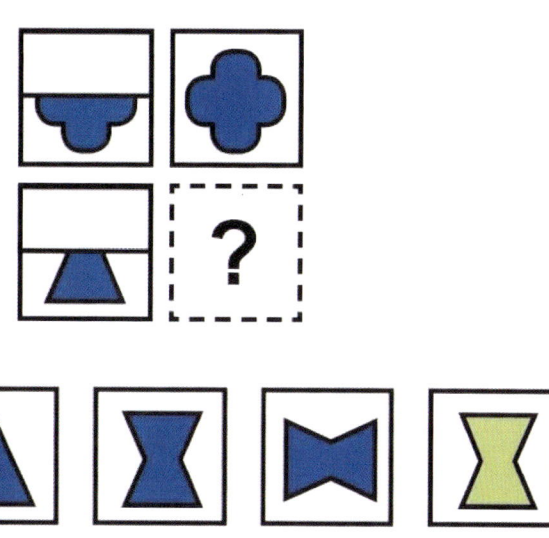

6

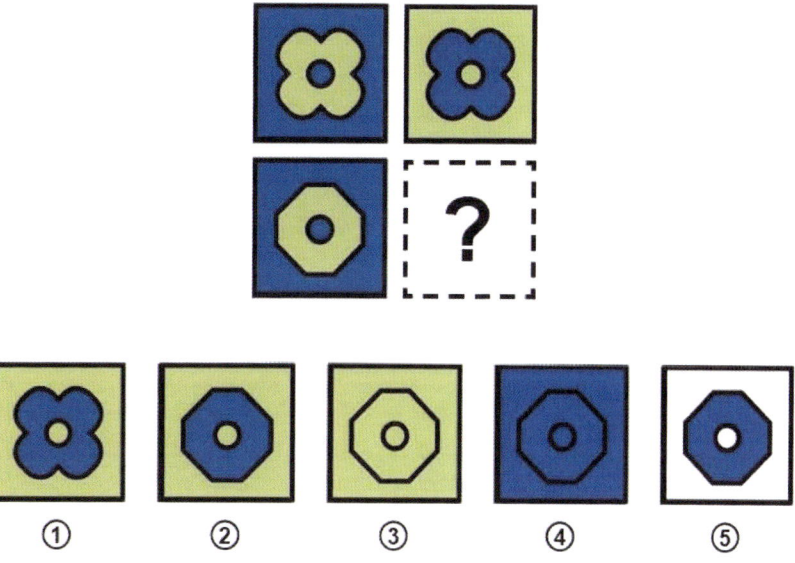

7

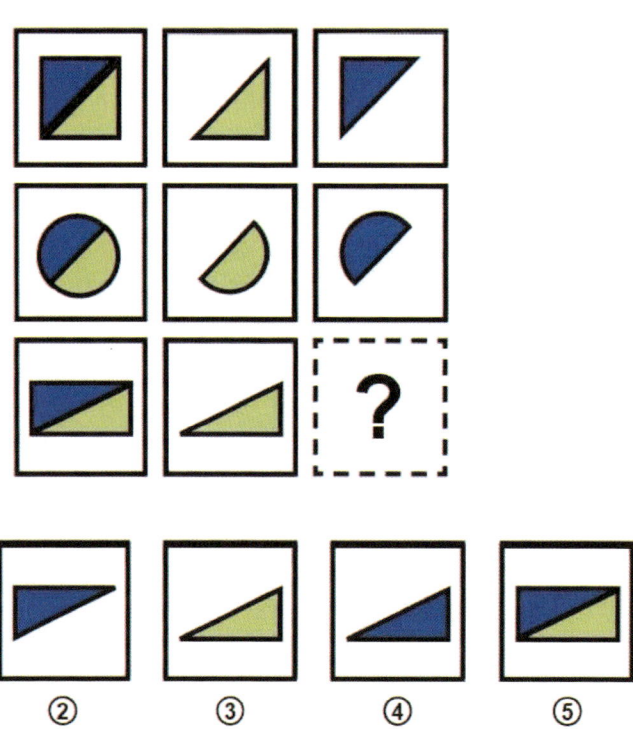

8

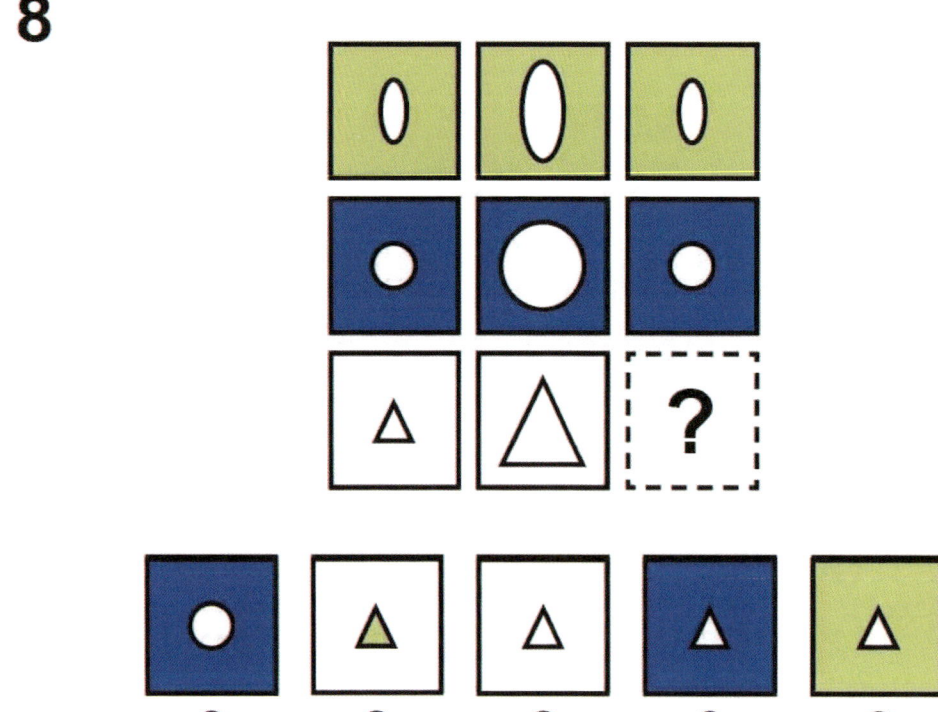

9

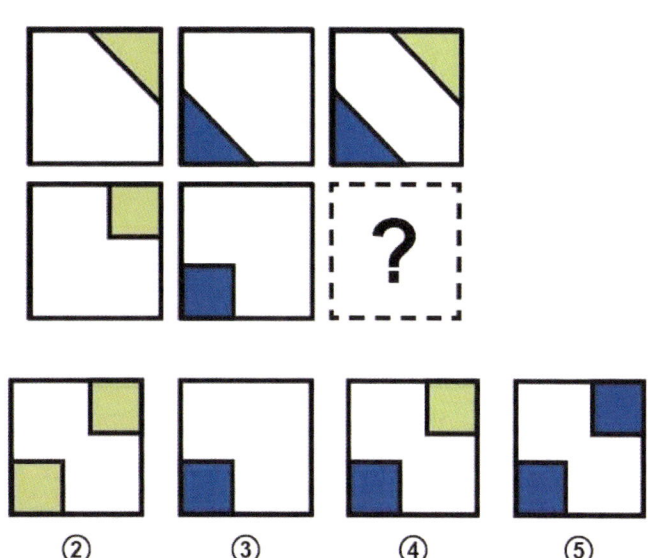

10

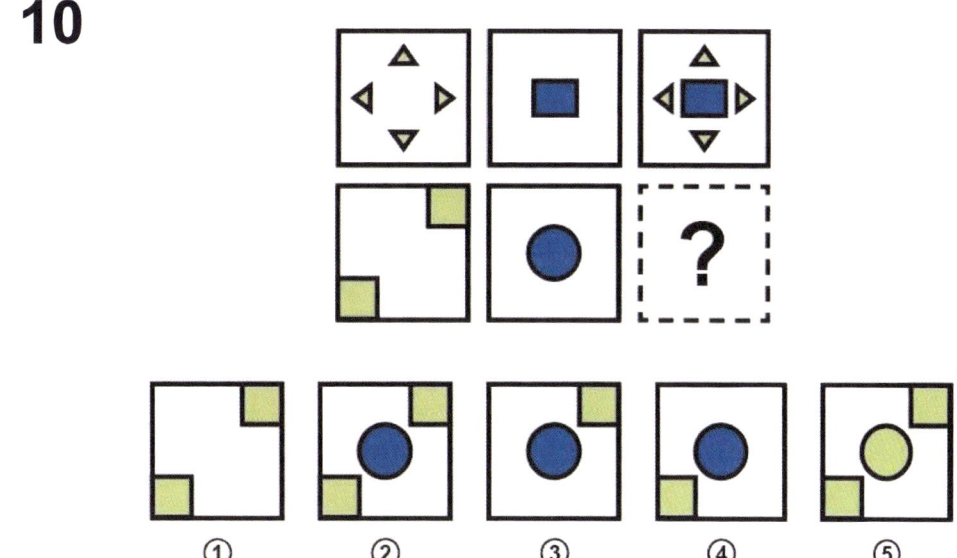

OLSAT Practice Test   30 minutes

Before beginning the test:
- Tear out the test prompts/instructions and answers. (Pages 105-109)
- Seat the child at a table with a practice test and pencil.
- Remove all other distractions and inform the child that he/she will be taking a test today.

During the test:
- Maintain a relaxed environment. Do not stress the child out during the test.
- Keep in mind that these 30 questions are to be done within **30 minutes**. Each child should not take longer than 1 minute for each question.
- Sit next to the child and read aloud the prompts. Pause after each question and give the chlid time to turn the page when necessary.

Scoring Guidelines
- Score the test by counting the total number of correct answers.
- When taking actual tests for gifted and talented programs, your child's score will most likely be scaled scores or percentile ranks which take into consideration other factors such as age or content.
- Please remember that these tests and scores do not indicate what your child will get in standardized gifted and talented tests and rather only serve as practice for the real exams. In fact, your child will most likely score higher on the actual tests than these practice tests.

OLSAT Practice Test   30 minutes

1.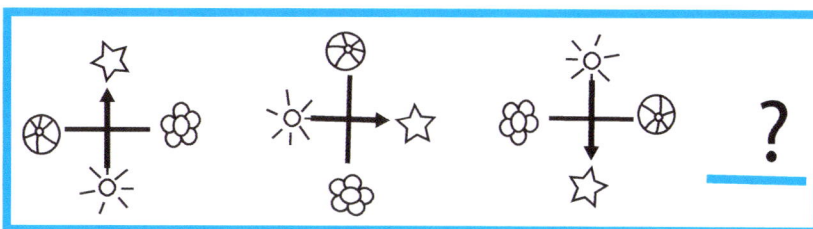

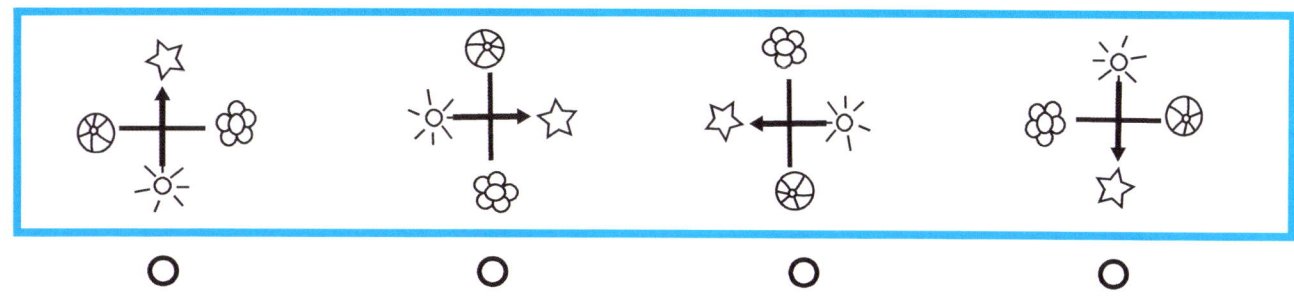

2.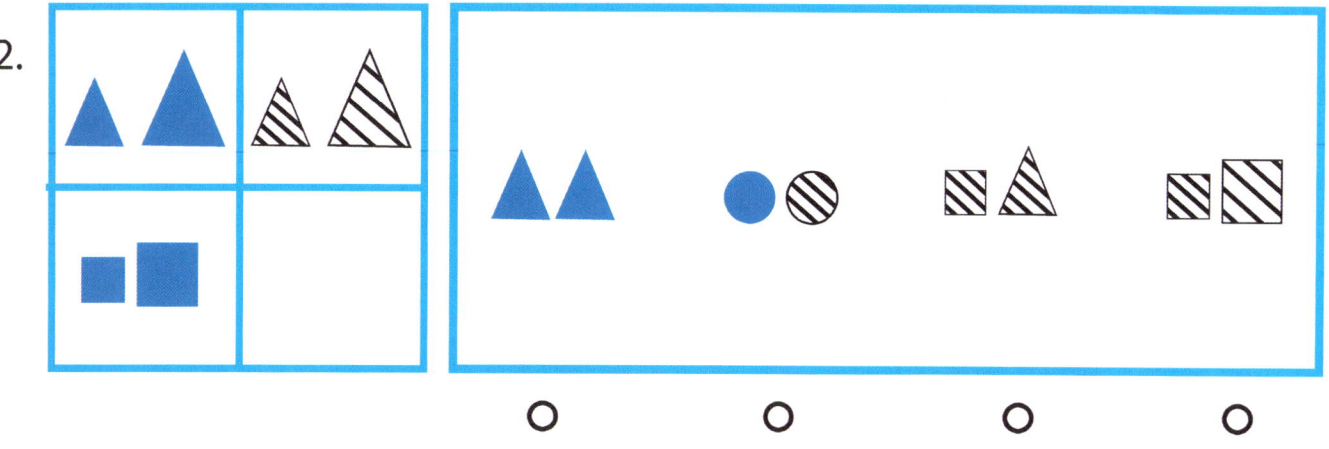

3.

OLSAT Practice Test 30 minutes

4.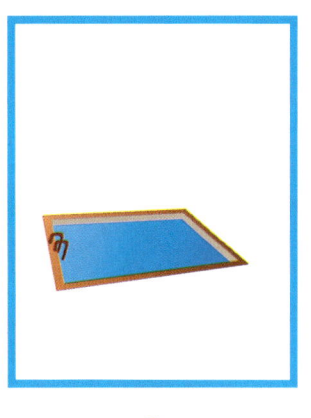
   ○ ○ ○ ○

5.
   ○ ○ ○ ○

6.
   ○ ○ ○ ○

OLSAT Practice Test 30 minutes

7.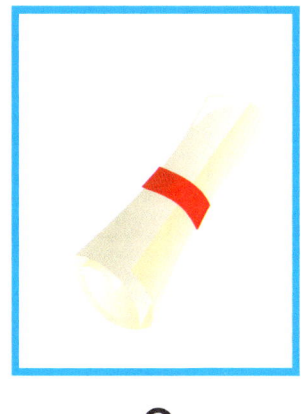
○ ○ ○ ○

8.
○ ○ ○ ○

9.
○ ○ ○ ○

OLSAT Practice Test   30 minutes

10.
   ○   ○   ○   ○

11.
   ○   ○   ○   ○

12. 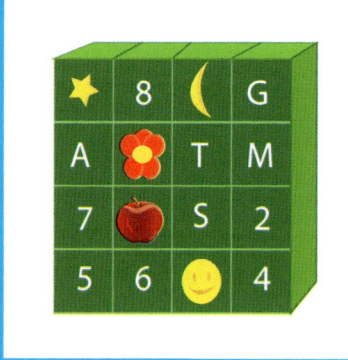   2   8   7   6
       ○   ○   ○   ○

OLSAT Practice Test   30 minutes

13.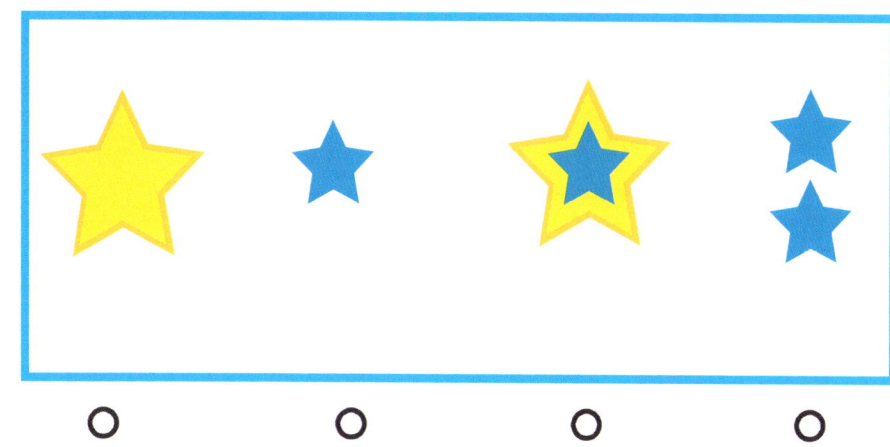

14.

15.

OLSAT Practice Test   30 minutes

16.
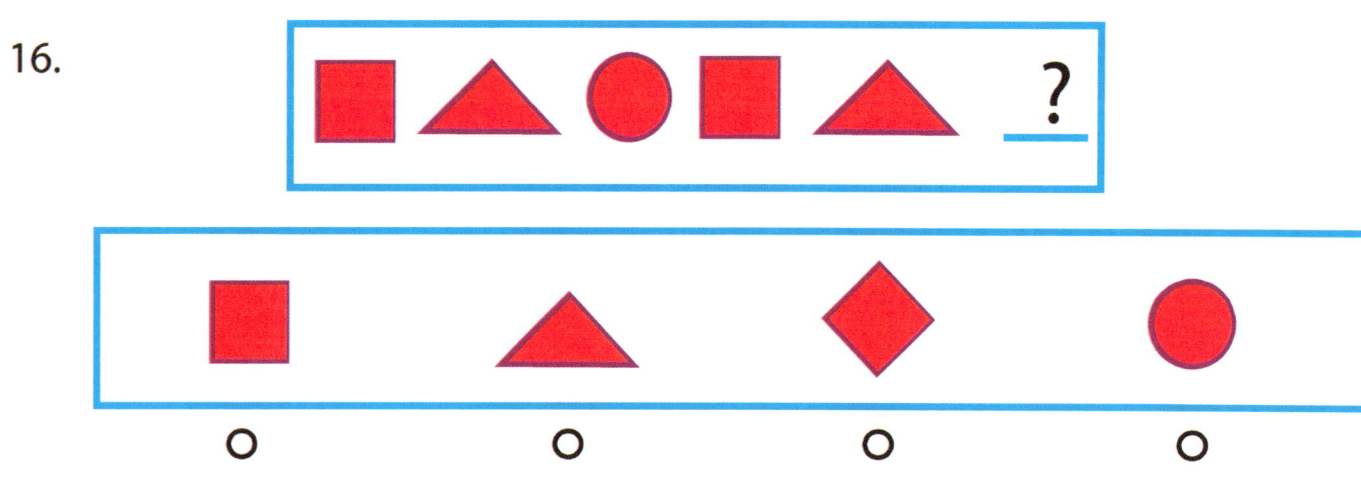

17.
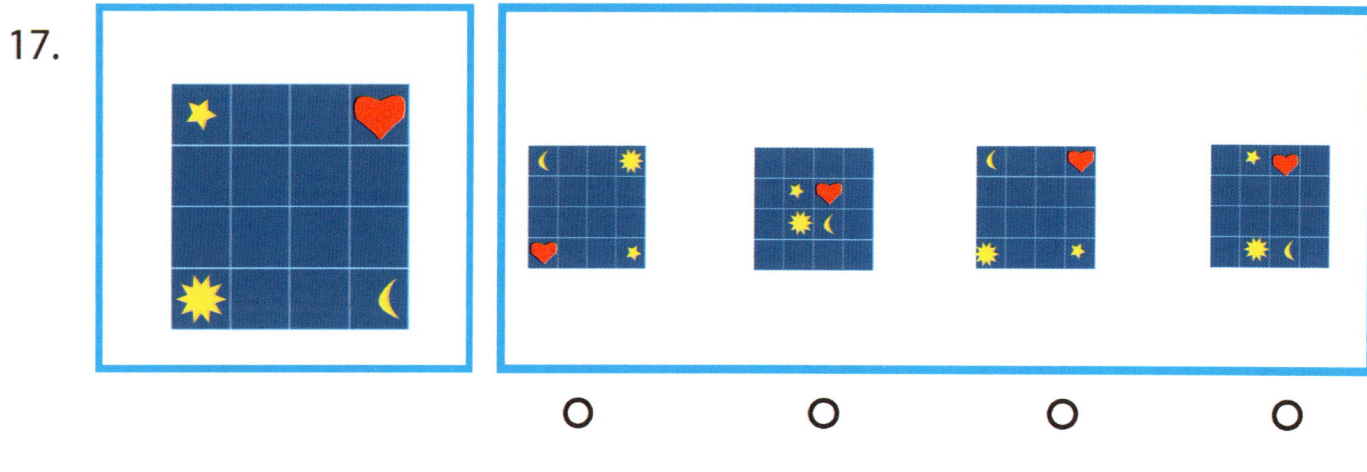

18.

19.
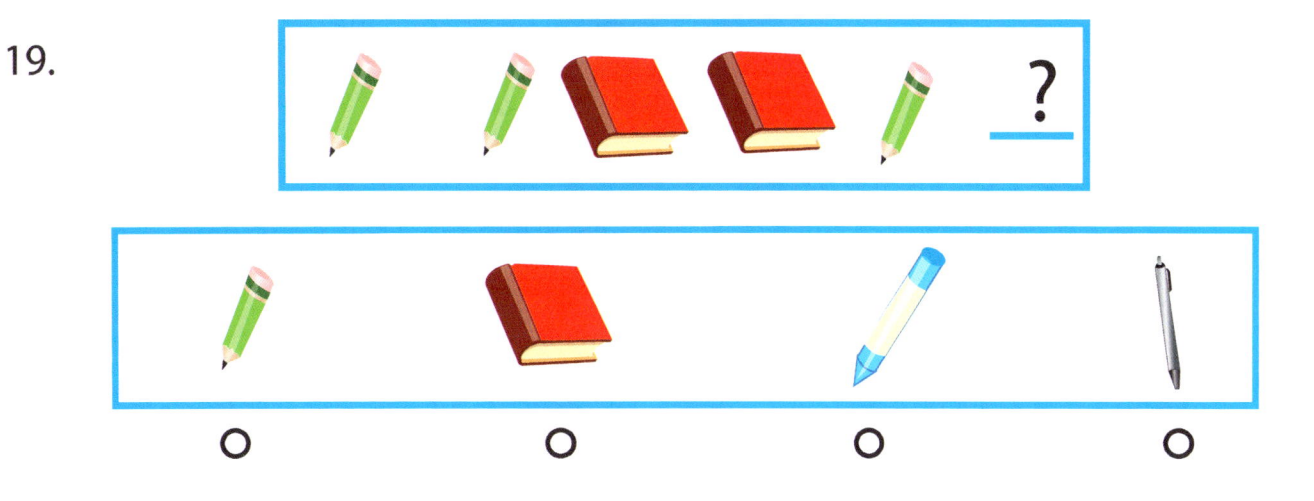

20.
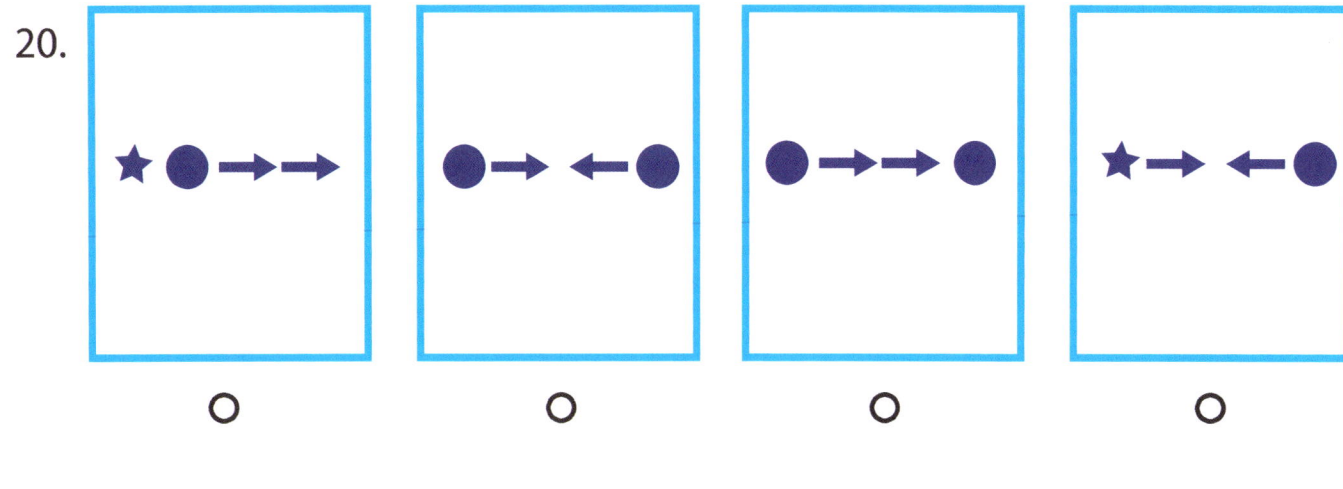

21.

OLSAT Practice Test 30 minutes

22.
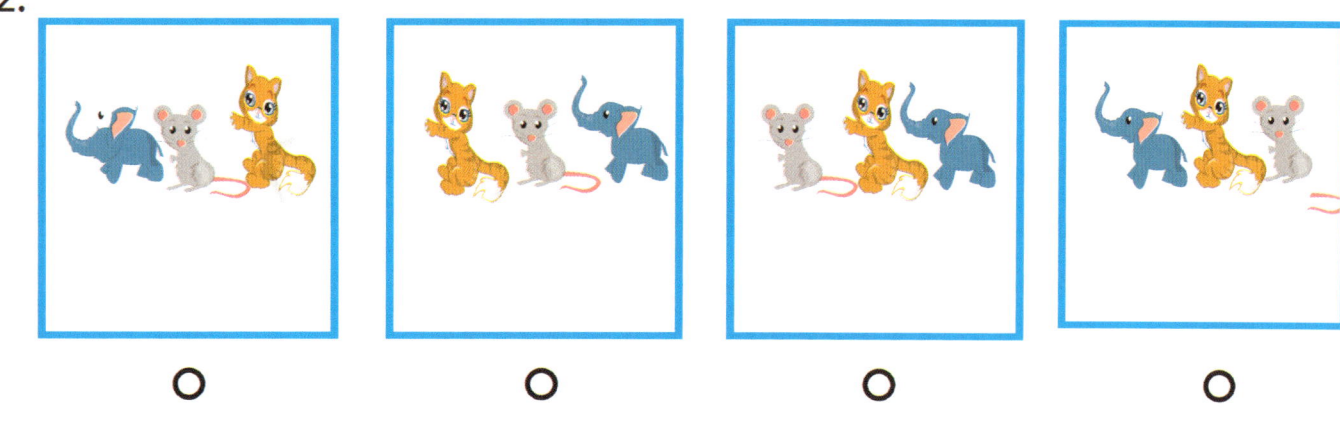

23.

24.

OLSAT Practice Test   30 minutes

25.

26.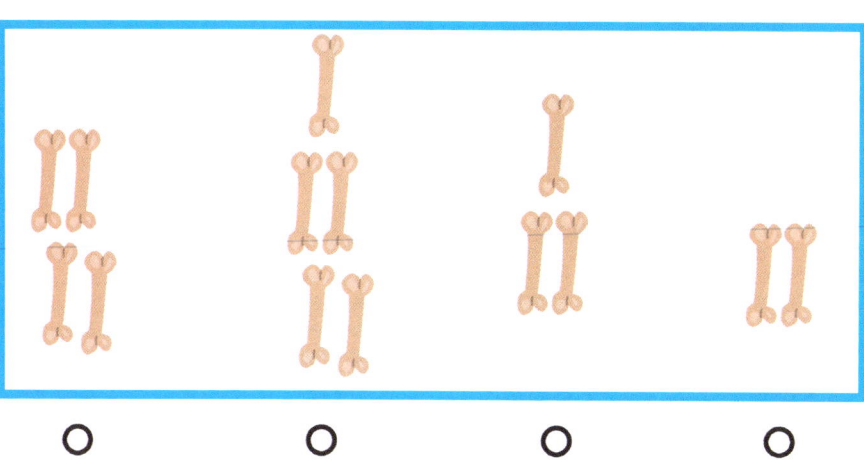

27.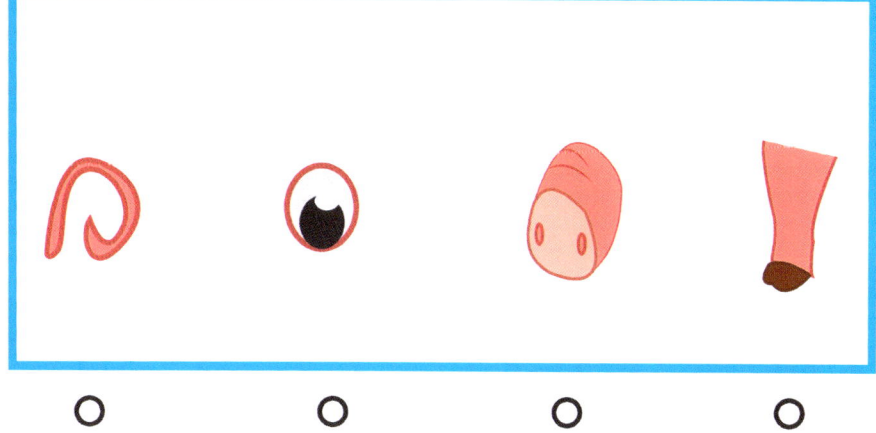

OLSAT Practice Test 30 minutes

28.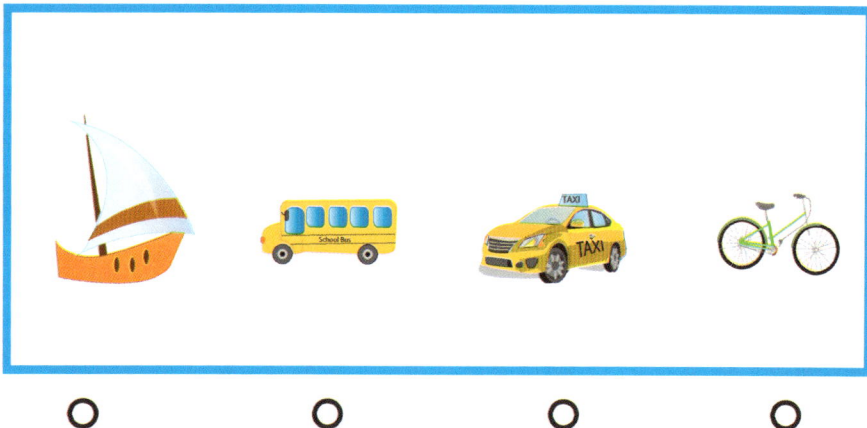

29.

30.

Practice Test   30 minutes

Parents: Before beginning, please tear off the pages 105-109 for the prompts. Read them to your child as he/she takes this test (page 94-104) and to check the answers.

Question #	Prompt	Answer
1	Look at the pattern in the first row. Fill in the circle under the picture that will complete the pattern.	3
2	Look at the set of shapes on the right. Fill in the circle under the picture that fits in the empty box so that the bottom row of shapes has the same relationship as the triangles on top.	4
3	Look at the row of pictures. Fill in the circle under the book that you can write an essay in.	1
4	Jack wants to swim and build a sand castle. Fill in the circle under the place where Jack should go.	1
5	Look at the row of pictures. Fill in the circle under the picture that people would put blinds or curtains, on.	1
6	Jack and Jill's mother needs to wash the dishes. Fill in the circle under the picture that shows where she will most likely wash the dishes.	4
7	Jill just graduated and received a certificate, a medal, and a trophy. Fill in the circle under the object that Jill did not get.	1

Practice Test   30 minutes

Question #	Prompt	Answer
8	Look at the row of pictures. Fill in the circle under the picture that shows a place for birds to rest on.	3
9	Look at the row of pictures. Fill in the circle under the picture that shows a girl wearing a dotted dress.	2
10	Jack only wants to eat something warm for lunch. Fill in the circle under the food that Jack definitely would not eat for lunch.	4
11	Look at the row of pictures. Fill in the circle under the person wearing a tie and no hat.	2
12	Look at the blocks. Fill in the circle under the number that is located on the block to the left of the apple.	3
13	Look at the big star and small star shown on the left. Fill in the circle under the picture with twice the number of little stars.	4
14	Look at the set of pictures in the big box on the left. Fill in the circle under the picture that best fits in the empty box so that the bottom row of ducks has the same relationship as the top row of flowers.	2

Practice Test — 30 minutes

Question #	Prompt	Answer
15	Look at the row of apple trees. Fill in the circle under the tree with the least number of apples.	3
16	Look at the pattern in the first row. Fill in the circle under the shape that best completes the pattern.	4
17	Look at the big box on the left. Fill in the circle under the box that shows the moon and the star switched.	3
18	Look at the birds on the left. Fill in the circle under the picture that shows only half the number of birds.	1
19	Look at the pattern on the top row. Fill in the circle under the picture that would best complete the pattern.	1
20	Look at the row of pictures. Fill in the circle under the picture with two circles and two arrows that are pointing each other.	2
21	There were four birds sitting on a branch. Then, one bird flew away. Fill in the circle under the picture that shows how many birds are left.	2

Practice Test   30 minutes

Question #	Prompt	Answer
22	Look at the row of animals. Fill in the circle under the picture that shows the cat immediately to the right of the elephant.	4
23	Jack has just come home from school. Fill in the circle under the picture that shows Jack what he would do first when he gets home.	4
24	Look at the whole pizza pie. Fill in the circle under the picture that shows the pie with one slice eaten.	2
25	Look at the row of pictures. Fill in the circle under the picture with a striped star inside a blue (solid) circle.	3
26	Look at the dogs on the left. Each dog needs to eat one bone. Fill in the circle under the picture that shows the number of bones Jack needs to feed all of them.	2
27	Look at the picture of the pig. Fill in the circle under the picture that shows a pig's snout or nose.	3
28	Jack needs to cross the river to get to school. Fill in the circle under the vehicle that Jack needs to ride in order to get to school.	1

Practice Test 30 minutes

Question #	Prompt	Answer
29	Look at the row of pictures. Fill in the circle under the picture that shows the mouse on the windowsill.	3
30	Look at the two seesaws on the first row. If one bear weighs the same as one car, how many bears weigh as much as two cars? Fill in the circle under the picture that would balance the scale.	3

Answer Key for P.1-28

Page #	Answer	Page #	Answer	Page #	Answer	Page #	Answer
P.1		P.8		P.15		P.22	
P.2		P.9	Q1 Answer 2 Q2 Answer 2 Q3 Answer 4	P.16		P.23	
P.3		P.10	Q4 Answer 3 Q5 Answer 3 Q6 Answer 4	P.17		P.24	Q1 Q2
P.4		P.11	Q7 Answer 1 Q8 Answer 4 Q9 Answer 1	P.18		P.25	
P.5		P.12	Q10 Answer 1 Q11 Answer 2 Q12 Answer 1	P.19		P.26	
P.6		P.13	Q13 Answer 3 Q14 Answer 2 Q15 Answer 2	P.20		P.27	
P.7		P.14	Q16 Answer 2 Q17 Answer 2 Q18 Answer 3	P.21		P.28	

Answer Key for P.29-56

Page #	Answer	Page #	Answer	Page #	Answer	Page #	Answer
P.29		P.36		P.43		P.50	Q3 Answer 4
							Q4 Answer 2
P.30		P.37		P.44		P.51	Q5 Answer 3
							Q6 Answer 2
P.31		P.38		P.45		P.52	Q7 Answer 4
							Q8 Answer 1
P.32		P.39		P.46		P.53	Q9 Answer 1
							Q10 Answer 2
P.33		P.40		P.47		P.54	Q11 Answer 3
							Q12 Answer 1
P.34		P.41		P.48		P.55	Q13 Answer 4
							Q14 Answer 3
P.35		P.42		P.49	Q1 Answer 2	P.56	Q15 Answer 2
					Q2 Answer 2		Q16 Answer 1

111 OLSAT Practice Test Pi For Kids Inc.©

Answer Key for P. 57-84

Page #	Answer	Page #	Answer	Page #	Answer	Page #	Answer
P.57	Q17 Answer 2 Q18 Answer 3	P.64		P.71		P.78	3 | 4 2 | 1
P.58	Q19 Answer 1 Q20 Answer 3	P.65		P.72		P.79	2 | 1 4 | 3
P.59	Q21 Answer 1 Q22 Answer 3	P.66		P.73		P.80	3 | 2 1 | 4
P.60		P.67		P.74	3 | 4 1 | 2	P.81	
P.61		P.68		P.75	2 | 3 4 | 1	P.82	
P.62		P.69		P.76	3 | 2 1 | 4	P.83	
P.63		P.70		P.77	2 | 1 4 | 3	P.84	

Answer Key for P. 85-93

Page #	Answer	Page #	Answer	Page #	Answer	Page #	Answer
P.85	(matching diagram)	P.93	Q9 Answer 4 Q10 Answer 2				
P.86	(matching diagram)						
P.87	(matching diagram)						
P.89	Q1 Answer 5 Q2 Answer 3						
P.90	Q3 Answer 3 Q4 Answer 2						
P.91	Q5 Answer 3 Q6 Answer 2						
P.92	Q7 Answer 2 Q8 Answer 3						

OLSAT PRACTICE TEST

Made in the USA
Lexington, KY
28 April 2016